PSYCHOLOGY PRACTITIONER GUIDEBOOKS

EDITORS

Arnold P. Goldstein, Syracuse University
Leonard Krasner, Stanford University & SUNY at Stony Brook
Sol L. Garfield, Washington University in St. Louis

THE PERSONALITY DISORDERS

Pergamon Titles of Related Interest

Dershimer COUNSELING THE BEREAVED

Fremouw/de Perczel/Ellis SUICIDE RISK: Assessment and Response Guidelines

Goldstein/Hersen HANDBOOK OF PSYCHOLOGICAL ASSESSMENT, Second Edition

Hersen/Last HANDBOOK OF CHILD AND ADULT PSYCHOPATHOLOGY: A Longitudinal Perspective

Kanfer/Goldstein HELPING PEOPLE CHANGE: A Textbook of Methods, Fourth Edition

Saigh POSTTRAUMATIC STRESS DISORDER: A Behavioral Approach to Assessment and Treatment

Related Journals
(Free sample copies available on request)

BEHAVIORAL ASSESSMENT
CLINICAL PSYCHOLOGY REVIEW
PERSONALITY AND INDIVIDUAL DIFFERENCES

THE PERSONALITY DISORDERS

A Psychological Approach to Clinical Management

IRA DANIEL TURKAT

Venice Hospital and
University of Florida College of Medicine

PERGAMON PRESS

Member of Maxwell Macmillan Pergamon Publishing Corporation
New York • Oxford • Beijing • Frankfurt •
São Paulo • Sydney • Tokyo • Toronto

142753

Pergamon Press Offices:

U.S.A.	Pergamon Press, Inc., Maxwell House, Fairview Park, Elmsford, New York 10523, U.S.A.
U.K.	Pergamon Press plc, Headington Hill Hall, Oxford OX3 0BW, England
PEOPLE'S REPUBLIC OF CHINA	Pergamon Press, 0909 China World Tower, No. 1 Jian Guo Men Wai Avenue, Beijing 100004, People's Republic of China
FEDERAL REPUBLIC OF GERMANY	Pergamon Press GmbH, Hammerweg 6, D-6242 Kronberg, Federal Republic of Germany
BRAZIL	Pergamon Editora Ltda, Rua Eça de Queiros, 346, CEP 04011, Paraiso, São Paulo, Brazil
AUSTRALIA	Pergamon Press Australia Pty Ltd., P.O. Box 544, Potts Point, NSW 2011, Australia
JAPAN	Pergamon Press, 8th Floor, Matsuoka Central Building, 1-7-1 Nishishinjuku, Shinjuku-ku, Tokyo 160, Japan
CANADA	Pergamon Press Canada Ltd., Suite 271, 253 College Street, Toronto, Ontario M5T 1R5, Canada

Library of Congress Cataloging in Publication Data

Turkat, Ira Daniel.
    The personality disorders : a psychological approach to clinical management / by Ira Daniel Turkat.
      p. cm. -- (Psychology practitioner guidebooks)
    Includes index.
    ISBN 0-08-036124-2:.—ISBN 0-08-036123-4 (pbk.) :
    1. Personality disorders—Treatment. I. Title. II. Series.
    [DNLM: 1. Personality Disorders. 2. Personality Disorders—
    —therapy. WM 190 T939p]
    RC554.T83 1990
    616.85'8–dc20   90-7243
                                                    CIP

Printing: 1 2 3 4 5 6 7 8 9   Year: 0 1 2 3 4 5 6 7 8 9

Printed in the United States of America

The paper used in this publication meets the minimum requirements of American National Standard for Information Sciences—Permanence of Paper for Printed Library Materials, ANSI Z39.48-1984

For my father and my brother, Michael and David.

Contents

Preface

My interest in the personality disorders can be traced indirectly to my humble beginnings as an undergraduate at the University of Vermont in the 1970s. While there, I became interested in (and in fact, quite excited about) behavior therapy. I spent much of my spare time reading the behavioral journals (which was relatively easy to do back then) and constantly questioning the faculty and doctoral students. I was fortunate indeed to have had such responsive teachers. I left for graduate school with great anticipation.

Perhaps the most critical event in my career came about during my freshman year in the Doctoral Program at the University of Georgia. I had just completed an initial interview which was videotaped. For the first time in my training, the supervising clinical faculty member sat down with me to critique my performance. I thought I had it all figured out. I knew which behavioral treatment techniques I would use. I was ready. I put on the tape.

After watching the tape for 30 seconds, the supervisor told me to shut it off. He then proceeded to tell me numerous other problems that this individual would evidence later on in the videotape as well as critical historical variables. None of these ideas had occurred to me. He then instructed me to turn the tape back on. He was right on all counts. The case turned out to be a paranoid personality disorder. The supervisor was Henry E. Adams.

Following training along these lines, I became interested in trying to learn how to formulate complex cases like personality disorders from a behavioral perspective. There was nothing in the literature that was of any help. Dr. Adams suggested I spend my doctoral internship with Victor Meyer at the Middlesex Hospital Medical School at the University of London. While Dr. Meyer had an inordinately long list of people waiting to be his trainee, I was fortunate enough to be accepted to train with him.

During my training with Dr. Meyer, he repeatedly told me to, "throw away all the techniques you have learned." He emphasized not to do anything until a proper formulation of the case was developed. With a proper formulation, the likelihood of devising appropriate intervention is increased. We never spoke about personality disorders at that time (pre-DSM-III [Diagnostic and Statistical Manual of Mental Disorders, Third Edition]) but the lessons were powerful.

Following the completion of my dissertation and clinical training with Dr. Adams, and my internship training, I joined the faculty at Vanderbilt University as an Assistant Professor in the Department of Psychology and Department of Medicine. In this same year DSM-III was published and as I began to acquaint myself with the new diagnostic scheme, I was amazed at how frequently I was seeing personality disorder cases clinically. Given the lack of useful scientific literature on the personality disorders, as well as the total absence of discussion about their clinical management by behavior therapists (many of whom still argue that personality disorders do not exist) I began spending much time reading basic psychopathology and personality literature. As my clinical experience with these cases increased, I decided to begin publishing my thoughts on these disorders. At the same time, I began to tackle a different research problem: studying the paranoid personality.

It is now 1990 and I have learned many things about these disorders. Perhaps the most important is that I have learned how much I still do not know. The fact that the learning experience is continuous is what helps to make the personality disorders so interesting to me.

What I present in this text represents growth in my clinical views and experience. My research with paranoid personality disorder is best exemplified by studies documenting how difficult it is to study the suspicious individual (e.g., Turkat & Banks, 1987; Thompson-Pope & Turkat, 1989).

With the advent of DSM-III-R (revised edition) and the degree of diagnostic overlap that occurs amongst the personality disorders, it seems to be getting harder and harder to be diagnostically clear with the system. This is because so many of the cases are most appropriately diagnosed as "personality disorder not otherwise specified," representing multiple traits across categories. Nevertheless, I believe the general framework of a formulation-based approach provides a firm foundation for tackling these difficulties.

Scientific evidence to support the effectiveness of treatment for personality disorders has yet to appear. I hope that the present volume will contribute somewhat toward our eventual achievement of this goal.

Ira Daniel Turkat, Ph.D.
Venice, Florida
April, 1990

Part I
Basic Guidelines and Initial Considerations

Chapter 1
Introduction to the Text

The personality disorders represent one of the most important, least understood, and most controversial categories of psychopathology (Liebowitz, Stone, & Turkat, 1986). Their importance is quickly revealed when one considers epidemiologic evidence: Approximately 50% of psychopathologic cases receive a personality disorder diagnosis (Turkat & Levin, 1984). The controversy surrounding them is highlighted by the frequent and significant modifications made in official diagnostic criteria despite the absence of appropriate research data. All told, the personality disorders present a significant challenge to the field of mental health.

The absence of research data to guide intervention leaves the clinician to choose between implementing treatments of unknown validity or not intervening at all. Neither option is desirable. Forced to attempt to treat troubled (and troubling) personality disorder cases without the benefit of scientific study, clinicians must rely on their experience and/or that of other clinicians. Too often the clinical literature lacks useful synopses on the management of personality disorder cases. For all of these reasons, the idea for this book was conceived.

THE PLAN OF THE BOOK

The book is organized in the following manner. Chapter 2 provides a review of the American Psychiatric Association's (APA) attempts to specify the various types of personality disorders. It offers summaries of the personality disorder sections of the DSM-I (APA, 1952), DSM-II (APA, 1968), and DSM-III (APA, 1980). The DSM-III-R (APA, 1987) criteria are discussed later in the text.

Chapter 3 is an introduction to the psychological approach adopted for conceptualization and management of the personality disorders. The approach is described in general terms with specific guidelines for clinical application. Chapter 4 then provides clinical illustrations of the approach as applied to diverse personality disorder cases.

Chapters 5 through 7 focus on specific personality disorders according to the "cluster" scheme of DSM-III-R (APA, 1987). They include discussions of *Cluster A* (paranoid personality disorder, schizoid personality disorder, and schizotypal personality disorder), *Cluster B* (antisocial personality disorder, borderline personality disorder, histrionic personality disorder, and narcissistic personality disorder), and *Cluster C* (avoidant personality disorder, obsessive compulsive personality disorder, dependent personality disorder, and passive aggressive personality disorder). Clinical experience with the DSM-III-R personality disorders is reviewed in relation to application of the psychological approach described earlier.

Chapter 8 outlines the specific responsibilities of the clinician in regard to generating scientific knowledge about the personality disorders. Concluding comments are provided in chapter 9.

The practitioner reading this book should come away with a firm grounding in the diagnosis, formulation, and management of the personality disorders as well as an approach to contributing to the body of literature on these important, poorly understood, and controversial pathologies.

Chapter 2

Personality Disorder
Diagnostic Schemes

In 1952, the APA published the first edition of the *Diagnostic and Statistical Manual of Mental Disorders* (DSM-I). Within it, the personality disorders were introduced officially into the diagnostic literature for psychopathology. Over the next 35 years, numerous modifications of this original classification scheme have been implemented. This chapter reviews these developments.

DSM-I

The DSM-I indicates that the personality disorders were organized into four categories: (a) personality pattern disturbances, (b) personality trait disturbances, (c) sociopathic personality disturbances, and (d) special symptom reactions. However, examination of the first official document of the APA on psychopathology classification reveals a fifth character disorder category: transient situational personality disorders. Within each of the five nosologic units, several disorders were detailed. In all, over 25 different types of personality disorders were proposed (see Table 2.1).

The DSM-I conceptualized the broad class of personality as

> characterized by developmental defects or pathological trends in the personality structure, with minimal subjective anxiety, and little or no sense of distress. In most instances, the disorder is manifested by a lifelong pattern of action or behavior, rather than by mental or emotional symptom. (APA, 1952, p. 34)

Specific subcategories were prepared on the basis of general clinical description, theory regarding personality development dynamics, and need for nosologic flexibility. The personality pattern disturbances were conceptualized as "deep-seeded disturbances, with little room for re-

5

Table 2.1. DSM-I Personality Disorders

Personality Pattern Disturbances	Personality Trait Disturbances	Sociopathic Personality Disturbances	Special Symptom Reactions	Transient Situational Personality Disorders
1. Inadequate personality	1. Emotionally unstable personality	1. Antisocial reaction	1. Learning disturbances	1. Transient situational personality disturbance
2. Schizoid personality	2. Passive aggressive personality	2. Dyssocial reaction	2. Speech disturbances	2. Gross stress reaction
3. Cyclothymic personality	3. Compulsive personality	3. Sexual deviation	3. Enuresis	3. Adult situational reaction
4. Paranoid personality	4. Personality trait disturbance, other	4. Addiction – alcoholism	4. Somnambulism	4. Adjustment reaction of infancy
		5. Addiction – drug	5. Other	5. Adjustment reaction of childhood habit
				6. Adjustment reaction of childhood conduct
				7. Adjustment reaction of childhood neurotic traits
				8. Adjustment reaction of adolescence
				9. Adjustment reaction of late life

Note: From American Psychiatric Association: *Diagnostic and statistical manual of mental disorders*. Washington, DC, American Psychiatric Association, 1952. Reprinted with permission.

6

gression" (APA, 1952, p. 34). The personality trait disturbances and sociopathic personality disturbances were viewed differently. Individuals suffering from these problems were thought to "regress to a lower level of personality, organization and function without development of psychosis" (APA, 1952, pp. 34–35) when experiencing stress. The taxonomic unit of special symptom reactions was provided to permit flexibility in diagnosis. Finally, the transient situational personality disorders were listed to capture "an acute symptom response to a situation without apparent underlying personality disturbance" (APA, 1952, p. 40).

In reviewing this first official attempt by the American Psychiatric Association to classify personality pathology, the reader should note several points. First, there is evident willingness to propose a broad range of character disorders. Second, several of the original categories have survived (in some modified form) 30-odd years of DSM editions (e.g., passive aggressive personality disorder). Third, the influence of psychoanalytic concepts (e.g., regression) in certain proposals should be noted.

DSM-II

In 1968, the second edition of the DSM was published. With it, the nosologic unit for characterizing disorders of personality changed considerably.

Table 2.2 lists the DSM-II personality disorders. It shows that the original description of 27 character pathologies was reduced to 12 disorders; in addition, some DSM-I pathologies were eliminated and certain disorders were shifted to categories other than personality disturbance categories (e.g., sexual deviation). Several new proposals

Table 2.2. DSM-II Personality Disorders

Paranoid personality disorder
Cyclothymic personality disorder
Schizoid personality disorder
Explosive personality disorder
Obsessive compulsive personality disorder
Hysterical personality disorder
Asthenic personality disorder
Antisocial personality disorder
Passive aggressive personality disorder
Inadequate personality disorder
Other specific types of personality disorder
Unspecified personality disorder

Note: From American Psychiatric Association: *Diagnostic and statistical manual of mental disorders, second edition*. Washington, DC, American Psychiatric Association, 1968. Reprinted with permission.

were offered (e.g., asthenic personality disorder). Further, the nature of personality disorder conceptualization did not remain static. The DSM-II described personality disorders as "deeply ingrained maladaptive patterns of behavior that are perceptibly different in quality from psychotic and neurotic symptoms. Generally, these are life-long patterns, often recognized by the time of adolescence or earlier" (APA, 1968, p. 42). Subcategories contained short descriptions of approximately one paragraph in length, similar to their treatment in DSM-I. For example, the cyclothymic personality (also referred to as *affective personality*) was characterized by

> recurring and alternating periods of depression and elation. Periods of elation may be marked by ambition, warmth, enthusiasm, optimism, and high energy. Periods of depression may be marked by worry, pessimism, low energy, and a sense of futility. These mood variations are not readily attributable to external circumstances. If possible, the diagnosis should specify whether the mood is characteristically depressed, hypomanic, or alternating. (APA, 1968, p. 42)

In contrast to the characterization provided for the cyclothymic personality disorder, the description of the asthenic personality was limited to a solitary sentence: "This behavior pattern is characterized by easy fatigability, low energy level, lack of enthusiasm, marked incapacity for enjoyment, and oversensitivity to physical and emotional stress" (APA, 1968, p. 42).

Lack of specificity was evident in a variety of DSM-II personality pathology descriptions. Perhaps the most striking example was the description of the inadequate personality disorder:

> This behavior pattern is characterized by ineffectual responses to emotional, social, intellectual and physical demands. While the patient seems neither physically nor mentally deficient, he does manifest inadaptability, ineptness, poor judgement, social instability, and lack of physical and emotional stamina. (APA, 1968, p. 44)

Reaction to the DSM-II was hostile and dramatic, particularly in some circles in clinical psychology. Attacks on the DSM-II were made frequently and intensely regarding its lack of reliability and validity evidence, its clinical ineffectiveness, and its political implications. Offered during a time of rapid cultural, political, and social reform in the Western world, the shortcomings of DSM-II helped to fuel the rivalry between psychiatry and clinical psychology. The stage was set for a radical departure from the existing format of psychiatric diagnostic nosology.

DSM-III

To their credit, the authors of DSM-III did not consider their conceptualizations of mental disorders to be definitive. However, their proposals required that certain criteria, identifying specific symptoms, must be met for a disorder to be placed in a taxonomic classification. This was a considerable advance over the DSM-II, which forced diagnoses to be made by matching general descriptions of disorders to patients.

The fact that clinical psychologists were extremely dissatisfied with the DSM-II should not mask the considerable dissatisfaction that existed within psychiatry. Many efforts related to taxonomic issues had been developing within psychiatry; these had important implications for subsequent conceptualization of the personality disorders.

One of these was the work of the World Health Organization (WHO). Approximately every 10 years the WHO revises the International Classification of Diseases (ICD). The ICD includes a small section of psychiatric and behavioral dysfunctions, reflected in the ninth edition of ICD (ICD-9) published in 1979. Several years of work on psychiatric taxonomy had occurred prior to the ICD-9 publication. However, within American psychiatry, as early as 1974 the APA appointed a task force on nomenclature and statistics to revise DSM-II. The goals of this task force were to create a nosologic system that would be compatible with ICD-9 but would also meet other criteria. These included being clinically useful, atheoretical, reliable, and acceptable to both clinicians and researchers. In spite of this aim, American psychiatry was not satisfied with the final product of ICD-9.

Other developments in the 1970s were also influential. In that decade, investigators in the Department of Psychiatry at Washington University in St. Louis were creating a new set of diagnostic criteria to be used in psychiatric research. These came to be known as the Feighner Criteria (Feighner, Robbins, & Guze, 1972). This set described a small number of disorders that the authors believed had sufficient validity evidence (e.g., antisocial personality disorder, alcoholism, mania) to be described authoritatively.

Toward the later part of the decade, the Feighner Criteria were expanded by Spitzer (chairman of the DSM-III) and his associates at the New York State Psychiatric Institute of Columbia University. These came to be known as the Research Diagnostic Criteria (RDC). These criteria eventually led to a variety of diagnostic instruments, such as the Schedule for Affective and Schizophrenic Disorders (SADS; Endicott & Spitzer, 1978) and the Diagnostic Interview Schedule (DIS; Robins,

Helzer, Croughan, & Ratcliff, 1981). Each of these was evaluated for various reliability and validity issues.

Thus, in reviewing the development of the DSM-III, one can see that it emerged from a variety of sources. First, there was significant dissatisfaction with DSM-II. Second, the research base of the Feighner Criteria was introduced into the literature. Third, the Feighner Criteria were extended, becoming the Research Diagnostic Criteria. Fourth, there was pressure to expand the ICD-9 psychiatry section. Finally, the development of research-based instruments for diagnoses contributed to the impetus for substantial modification of the official nosology of psychiatric disorders in America.

In 1980, the APA published the DSM-III. In this version, five major characteristics appeared. First, there was an emphasis on descriptive features. In other words, the system attempted to be atheoretical and to emphasize presenting symptoms and not presumed etiology. Further, with a focus on descriptive features and the phenomenology of the disorder, the DSM-III minimized the amount of inferences that needed to be made for taxonomic categorization.

Second, an attempt was made in the DSM-III to provide a comprehensive description of individual disorders. This included not only a specification of essential information but also related details of important extraclassification attributes. For example, age of onset, course, impairment, complications, predisposing factors, prevalence, sex ratio, familial patterns, and other points of information were provided in addition to specific requirements for diagnosis. Further, several new categories were proposed (even when much of the aforementioned information was lacking).

A third major characteristic was that particular diagnostic criteria were specified for each type of psychopathology. These included several types of information, such as presence of key symptoms, a subset of additional symptoms, duration of symptoms, and exclusion criteria (presence/absence of certain symptoms). Although taxonomic criteria were specified, clinical judgment was still required to determine whether the necessary diagnostic criteria were met in any particular patient.

A fourth major attribute of the DSM-III was that the system focused on disorders and not individuals. The DSM-III stated that an individual may have many characteristics and pointed out that it is inaccurate and potentially demeaning to categorize and label persons. This attitude in print helped to diminish many concerns over possible misuse of classification.

Finally, a major characteristic of DSM-III is that it is multiaxial. This is an important distinction between the DSM-III and the preceding DSM issues. The multiaxial system grew out of the WHO's field trials for the ICD-9. Inherent in the multiaxial diagnostic concept is that several facets of a presenting problem exist and that related circumstances are often clinically relevant. In this sense, a multiaxial diagnosis assumes a more comprehensive description and in some cases may help improve diagnostic agreement by separating different dimensions of psychopathology. For purposes of this text, the critical aspect of the multiaxial system is that an entire axis (Axis II) was devoted to the personality disorders. Thus, every case was to be evaluated in terms of whether significant personality disturbances were evident.

Table 2.3 presents the DSM-III personality disorder categories. These show that several personality pathologies from DSM-II were retained (paranoid, schizoid, obsessive compulsive, hysterical, antisocial, passive aggressive). However, a variety of DSM-II personality disorder types were eliminated. These included the cyclothymic, explosive, asthenic, and inadequate. Further, some name changes occurred. For example, the hysterical personality disorder was now referred to as the histrionic personality disorder. Similarly, the identifier for obsessive compulsive personality disorder was shortened to compulsive personality disorder.

In DSM-III, personality traits were defined as "enduring patterns of perceiving, relating to, and thinking about the environment and one's self, and are exhibited in a wide range of important social and personal contexts" (APA, 1980, p. 305). This definition rests on the assumption that all individuals have personality traits. Thus, it is implied that one can have a "normal" compulsive personality. However, the DSM-III notes that "it is only when personality traits are inflexible and maladaptive and cause either significant impairment in social or occupational

Table 2.3.   DSM-III Personality Disorders

Antisocial personality disorder
Avoidant personality disorder
Borderline personality disorder
Compulsive personality disorder
Dependent personality disorder
Histrionic personality disorder
Narcissistic personality disorder
Paranoid personality disorder
Passive aggressive personality disorder
Schizoid personality disorder
Schizotypal personality disorder
Mixed personality disorder
Atypical personality disorder
Other personality disorder

Note: From American Psychiatric Association: *Diagnostic and statistical manual of mental disorders, third edition*. Washington, DC, American Psychiatric Association, 1980. Reprinted with permission.

functioning or subjective distress that they constitute personality disorders" (p. 305).

The advantage of this conceptualization is its differentiation between normal and abnormal personalities. The disadvantage is that the judgments of what constitutes "inflexible," "maladaptive," and "significant impairment" lead to reductions in diagnostic reliability. Finally, personality disorders are viewed as being present by the time of adolescence or earlier and continue on throughout adult life. In other words, they do not appear as transient symptoms.

To illustrate the change in personality pathology descriptions, the criteria in DSM-III for both schizoid personality disorder and paranoid disorders are listed in Table 2.4. The schizoid personality has six specific criteria that must be met in order for the diagnosis to be given. However, the DSM-III does not specify how these criteria are to be met. For example, what exactly qualifies as a "close friendship" (which is an important criterion for schizoid pathology description)?

In contrast, the paranoid personality disorder, which has four major criteria for diagnosis, has a variety of ways to meet a specific criterion. For example Part A, which focuses on suspiciousness and mistrust, can be met by three of eight possible signs. Both Criterion B and Criterion C require at least two of four attributes. Again, the methods for meeting specific criteria are not available. For example, what exactly qualifies as "lack of a true sense of humor"?

Although significant advancement has occurred in criterion specification, considerable problems in diagnostic reliability remain. The DSM-III field trials (APA, 1980) indicated that diagnostic reliability for the personality disorders was relatively unacceptable (the highest kappa coefficient of agreement achieved was .65). It is of major interest that in the DSM-III field trials (which included hundreds of patients across North America), 50% to 60% of the patients received personality disorder diagnoses (across Phase I and Phase II of the field trials).

DSM-III-R

Three years after the publication of DSM-III, the APA began work on revising its 1980 product. As noted by Spitzer and Williams in their 1987 introduction to DSM-III-R, research and clinical experience with the DSM-III was beginning to disclose significant problems with it. These included practical difficulties with the criteria, lack of validation for certain criteria, and other issues of accuracy and conceptual clarity. Spitzer and Williams (1987) also noted that about this time, the ICD-10 was being prepared and thus efforts from the APA to participate in that

Table 2.4. DSM-III Diagnostic Criteria for Paranoid and Schizoid Personality Disorders

Diagnostic Criteria for Paranoid Personality Disorder
The following are characteristics of the individual's current and long-term functioning, are not limited to episodes of illness, and cause either significant impairment in social or occupational functioning or subjective distress.
A. Pervasive, unwarranted suspiciousness and mistrust of people as indicated by at least three of the following:
    1. Expectation of trickery or harm
    2. Hypervigilance, manifested by continual scanning of the environment for signs of threat, or taking unneeded precautions
    3. Guardedness or secretiveness
    4. Avoidance of accepting blame when warranted
    5. Questioning the loyalty of others
    6. Intense, narrowly focused searching for confirmation of bias, with loss of appreciation of total context
    7. Overconcern with hidden motives and special meanings
    8. Pathological jealousy
B. Hypersensitivity as indicated by at least two of the following:
    1. Tendency to be easily slighted and quick to take offense
    2. Exaggeration of difficulties, for example, "making mountains out of molehills"
    3. Readiness to counterattack when any threat is perceived
    4. Inability to relax
C. Restricted affectivity as indicated by at least two of the following:
    1. Appearance of being "cold" and unemotional
    2. Pride taken in always being objective, rational, and unemotional
    3. Lack of a true sense of humor
    4. Absence of passive, soft, tender, and sentimental feelings
D. Not due to another mental disorder such as schizophrenia or a paranoid disorder

Diagnostic Criteria for Schizoid Personality Disorder
The following are characteristic of the individual's current and long-term functioning, are not limited to episodes of illness, and cause either significant impairment in social or occupational functioning or subjective distress.
A. Emotional coldness and aloofness, and absence of warm, tender feelings for others
B. Indifference to praise or criticism or to the feelings of others
C. Close friendships with no more than one or two persons, including family members
D. No eccentricities of speech, behavior, or thought characteristic of schizotypal personality disorder
E. Not due to a psychotic disorder such as schizophrenia or paranoid disorder
F. If under 18, does not meet the criteria for schizoid disorder of childhood or adolescence

Note: From American Psychiatric Association: *Diagnostic and statistical manual of mental disorders, third edition.* Washington, DC, American Psychiatric Association, 1980. Reprinted with permission.

process coincided with work toward the DSM-III-R. In addition, these authors observed that in the 7 years following the publication of DSM-III, over 2,000 articles about it had appeared in the scientific literature. Accordingly, the Board of Trustees of the APA approved the appointment of a work group to revise DSM-III. Twenty advisory committees with over 200 members were formed. In 1985, a draft of

DSM-III-R, entitled *DSM-III-R in Development,* was distributed to interested professionals, and critical review was invited. A similar process occurred the following year, and three national field trials were conducted on the proposed DSM-III-R criteria.

There is no doubt that the personality disorder section of the DSM-III-R had changed. Although the personality disorders that were specified in DSM-III remained, they were classified into three clusters as shown in Table 2.5. The DSM-III-R describes Cluster A personality disorders as those in which individuals appear "odd or eccentric." Examples include the paranoid and schizotypal personality disorders. Cluster B referred to those disorders in which dramatic, emotional, or erratic features appeared. Thus, for example, individuals classified as having borderline personality disorder or histrionic personality disorder were listed.

Finally, Cluster C included individuals who appeared anxious or fearful, such as those with the disorders labeled the avoidant personality and the passive aggressive personality. The DSM-III categories of mixed, atypical, and/or other personality disorders were now combined into a new category called *personality disorder not otherwise specified.*

As shown in Table 2.6, the specifics of diagnostic criteria were changed for several disorders. Although the general concepts underlying the personality pathologies remained, the changes in criteria, such as in the paranoid personality disorder (see Table 2.6), would have a significant effect on research. Utilizing this disorder as an example, as there has been little research on the paranoid personality disorder (Turkat, 1985), the changes in criterion specification are being affected by variables other than scientific evidence. How the current taxonomy of personality pathology will fare remains an empirical question.

Reviews of the currently accepted DSM-III-R personality disorders are provided in later sections of this book.

Table 2.5.   DSM-III-R Personality Disorder Clusters

Cluster A	Cluster B	Cluster C
Paranoid personality disorder	Antisocial personality disorder	Avoidant personality disorder
Schizoid personality disorder	Borderline personality disorder	Dependent personality disorder
Schizotypal personality disorder	Histrionic personality disorder	Obsessive compulsive personality disorder
	Narcissistic personality disorder	Passive aggressive personality disorder

Note: From American Psychiatric Association: *Diagnostic and statistical manual of mental disorders, third edition, revised.* Washington, DC, American Psychiatric Association, 1987. Reprinted with permission.

Table 2.6. DSM-III and DSM-III-R Criteria for Paranoid Personality Disorder

DSM-III Paranoid Personality Disorder

The following are characteristics of the individual's current and long-term functioning, are not limited to episodes of illness, and cause either significant impairment in social or occupational functioning or subjective distress.

A. Pervasive, unwarranted suspiciousness and mistrust of people as indicated by at least three of the following:
  1. Expectation of trickery or harm
  2. Hypervigilance, manifested by continual scanning of the environment for signs of threat, or taking unneeded precautions
  3. Guardedness or secretiveness
  4. Avoidance of accepting blame when warranted
  5. Questioning the loyalty of others
  6. Intense, narrowly focused searching for confirmation of bias, with loss of appreciation of total context
  7. Overconcern with hidden motives and special meanings
  8. Pathological jealousy
B. Hypersensitivity as indicated by at least two of the following:
  1. Tendency to be easily slighted and quick to take offense
  2. Exaggeration of difficulties, for example, "making mountains out of molehills"
  3. Readiness to counterattack when any threat is perceived
  4. Inability to relax
C. Restricted affectivity as indicated by at least two of the following:
  1. Appearance of being "cold" and unemotional
  2. Pride taken in always being objective, rational, and unemotional
  3. Lack of a true sense of humor
  4. Absence of passive, soft, tender, and sentimental feelings
D. Not due to another mental disorder such as schizophrenia or a paranoid disorder

DSM-III-R Paranoid Personality Disorder

A. A pervasive and unwarranted tendency, beginning by early adulthood and present in a variety of contexts, to interpret the actions of people as deliberately demeaning or threatening, as indicated by at least four of the following:
  1. Expects, without sufficient basis, to be exploited or harmed by others
  2. Questions, without justification, the loyalty or trustworthiness of associates
  3. Reads hidden, demeaning or threatening meanings into benign remarks or events, e.g., suspects that a neighbor put out trash early to annoy him or her
  4. Bears grudges or is unforgiving of insults or slights
  5. Is reluctant to confide in others because of unwarranted fear that information will be used against him or her
  6. Is easily slighted and quick to react with anger or to counterattack
  7. Questions, without justification, fidelity of spouse or sexual partner
B. Occurence not exclusively during the course of schizophrenia or delusional disorder

Note: From American Psychiatric Association: *Diagnostic and statistical manual of mental disorders, third edition & third edition, revised.* Washington, DC, American Psychiatric Association, 1980; 1987. Reprinted with permission.

Chapter 3

Introduction to the Psychological Approach

In this section, one approach to the formulation and modification of psychological disorders will be presented. There is no evidence to suggest that this approach is comparatively any better or worse from a scientific standpoint, in terms of its efficacy. However, there seem to be merits to it besides what the author might conceive of, as evidenced by its adoption by others (e.g., Malatesta, Aubachon, Bloomgarten, & Kowitt, 1989; Persons, 1989). Further, some have gone so far as to state that "Turkat and his colleagues have broken important new ground by developing an empirically based approach to the understanding and treatment of personality disorders" (Pretzer & Fleming, 1989, p. 106).

While appreciative of such optimism, I must disagree with Pretzer and Fleming's (1989) evaluation. At this point, all that can be claimed with confidence is that one approach to conceptualizing and treating psychological disorders has been described (e.g., Meyer & Turkat, 1979; Turkat & Meyer, 1982; Wolpe & Turkat, 1985) and applied to cases of personality pathology (e.g., Turkat & Maisto, 1985). Scientific evidence to support or refute the validity of the approach is lacking.

In collaboration with Meyer, I first described the psychological approach examined in this text in the 1970s (Meyer & Turkat, 1979). However, its roots rest with the following individuals, in terms of their influence on my training or their contributions to professional publications: Henry Adams, Victor Meyer, Monte B. Shapiro, and Joseph Wolpe.

THE TRIPARTITE NATURE OF CLINICAL WORK

The psychological approach can be broken into three major stages. First is the *initial interview*. Here the clinician develops a formulation of

16

the presenting phenomena as well as a psychiatric diagnosis. In the second stage, *clinical experimentation*, the clinician gathers evidence to test the validity of his or her thinking about the presenting phenomena. In the final stage, *modification methodology*, the therapist develops an intervention plan that is implemented and subjected to scrutiny.

Initial Interview

The purpose of the initial interview is to achieve two primary goals. First, the clinician aims to develop a formulation of the behavioral problems that the patient brings to the professional's office. Second, the practitioner aims to specify an appropriate diagnosis utilizing the DSM-III-R criteria (APA, 1987). It is important to clarify here the nature of and relationship between the formulation and the diagnosis.

In this text, a formulation is defined as a theory about a patient's difficulties that has the following three components:

1. A hypothesis about the relationship among the various problems of the individual.
2. Hypotheses about the etiology of the aforementioned difficulties.
3. Predictions about the patient's future behavior.

With this definition of a formulation, any conceptualization of the patient's difficulties that does not include components one, two, and three does not quality as a formulation (at least in this approach). To say that one has a formulation of a particular case, one must be able to specify how all three requirements have been met. It is important to realize that the formulation of the case refers to the nature in which the presenting phenomena appear (in the clinician's eyes) to organize, develop, and most likely unfold in the future. Diagnosis, on the other hand, particularly with our present state of knowledge, does not accomplish what a formulation does. Rather, the diagnosis is merely a shorthand description of various behaviors that often coexist in the same individual. In this sense, the diagnosis is merely descriptive, utilized for communication and classification purposes (Adams, 1981). As noted elsewhere (Turkat & Maisto, 1983), the diagnosis and formulation complement each other. They are not the same, nor should they be construed as being the same. It is particularly problematic when one uses a diagnosis as his or her "formulation." I find the term *diagnostic formulation* to be a confusing one.

Given the definition of a formulation presented above, it is clear that the clinician must adjust to the patient. In other words, having a standard approach for interacting with a client is an impediment to achieving the goals of developing a formulation and a diagnosis. To reach the goals of the initial interview, one must carefully observe the patient, listen intensely to his or her report, and begin to generate hypotheses about the presenting phenomena. Given the goal of constructing a theory (i.e., formulation) as well as a description (i.e., diagnosis), the process is one of continuous hypothesis testing. It is similar to the nature of scientific inquiry, as can be seen in Figure 3.1. Cars run on fuel. Science runs on hypotheses.

Some individuals question the need for making diagnostic statements. As mentioned before, it is imperative for scientific communication and classification that a similar diagnostic system be used by the various professionals in a field. The most widely used and accepted taxonomic system is that devised by the APA and published in the DSM. Although it contains many problems, this classification system appears to be the best we have. Further, as noted by others (Adams, 1981; Cattel, 1946), science in any field does not proceed without a reliable and valid classification system that is adhered to by the members of that profession.

A second reason for utilizing the diagnostic system, particularly with personality disorders, is that there is a class of clinical cases in which certain behavioral patterns coexist in the same individual (Turner & Turkat, 1988). Thus, knowing the diagnostic criteria can help the clinician test hypotheses, a process that can be useful in the development of a formulation. For example, knowing response patterns that often covary helps one to identify problem areas that the patient may not specify by his or her own report. Because the formulation has a

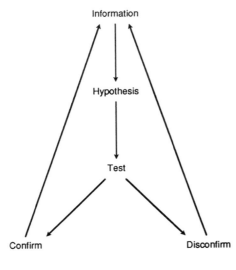

FIGURE 3.1. The nature of hypothesis testing.

criterion of accounting for all the patient's difficulties (via the hypothesis about their relationship to each other), knowledge of diagnostic criteria is helpful in many cases. Again, the diagnosis is not equivalent to the formulation; it is complementary.

Utilizing the tripartite definition of a case formulation, the clinician has much to accomplish in the initial interview. In my experience, few are able to meet these criteria in one interview. Further, mere gathering of information impedes the clinician's ability to formulate the case efficiently (Wolpe & Turkat, 1985). Nevertheless, guidelines for conducting the initial interview are presented below. These should not be followed in exact sequence. Rather, it is the clinician's hypotheses that guide the interview process (Turkat, 1986; 1987). Because of the nature of the phenomena we deal with in psychopathology, it is impossible to specify an exact route to apply to all cases. However, the reader should find the following information helpful in attempts to develop a formulation.

At the first meeting with a patient, my aim is to achieve both a formulation and diagnosis by the end of the initial interview. Ninety minutes is typically allocated to meeting these goals. It is critical to understand that the entire model presented here is highly dependent on the development of a formulation. Furthermore, the formulation dictates what the treatment plan will be. It is this connection between the formulation and the treatment approach that strongly differentiates a formulation-based approach from other approaches, such as the technologically oriented type of behavioral therapy practiced by so many (Turkat, 1982).

STEPS IN THE INITIAL INTERVIEW

In this section, the various steps usually engaged in to arrive at a formulation, are presented. These steps or stages are merely guidelines; they are not to be followed in exact sequence. Hypotheses and data determine the order of events. Given the current state of our knowledge regarding psychopathology, it is impossible to specify operationally precise decision routes. Nevertheless, the reader should find the guidelines below to be of some value.

Initial Interaction

As the therapist aims to develop a hypothesis about the presenting phenomena, he or she must collect data in order to make an inference.

Accordingly, as soon as the patient interacts with the therapist, *regardless of the nature of the interaction*, data are being presented, and the therapist attempts to organize the presenting data by means of a single hypothesis. Hence, the therapist carefully scrutinizes every action, word, appearance, and attribute that the patient presents. It does not matter if this information is developed in a telephone conversation, in the office lobby, in the hall, or in the treatment room. A simple example might prove useful.

The secretary reports that the initial interview will be somewhat delayed because the prospective patient is having difficulty signing the standard consent forms (to receive evaluation and treatment at the clinic). Accordingly, the therapist should contemplate the following: "Since there is seldom a problem with patients and consent forms, what type of individual would have concerns about this?" It is a fair inference to make that the person questioning the consent form is a guarded individual, particularly when it comes to revealing important personal aspects. In my experience, individuals who are this careful often have problems trusting others and frequently are suspicious in nature. The first hypothesis generated might be a diagnostic one: "Perhaps I am dealing with a paranoid personality disorder." It is important for the reader to understand that the hypothesis produced here may be wrong; further data will either confirm or deny its validity. However, what should be clear from the present example is how even minimal pieces of information are used as a data base to permit hypothesis generation (see Turkat, 1987). It is collecting information, creating hypotheses, and confirming or invalidating these ideas that characterize the psychological approach presented in this test.

Problem Specification

It is often useful to begin the initial interview by asking the general question, "What seems to be the problem?" Other helpful variations include "How can I help?" or "What has brought you to see me?" In developing the data base and/or testing hypotheses, the clinician should pay close attention to the patient's responses, then attempt to answer the following question: "Why did the patient present this first?" Both points need to be addressed. Naturally, the therapist is interested in a detailed description of what brings the client to his or her office for help. Typically, the patient complains about the most troubling problem first, but not always. However, *why* the individual chooses a particular problem as the first reply can be useful in understanding the patient's difficulties. For example, an attractive, well-groomed, styled, and immediately charming individual sits on the couch in the therapist's office.

In response to the first question the patient states, "I don't really think I need to be here but I came in order to satisfy my spouse." The therapist should ask him- or herself the following: "Is the spouse the problem, or is the patient's lack of identifying his or her own difficulties as worthy of clinical attention the problem?" Assume for the moment that the latter may be true; if so, are any particular categories suggested by the fact that the patient is attractive, charming, and insensitive to his or her own difficulties, yet comes to "get the spouse off his or her back?" Clearly, yes. Immediate hypotheses about psychopathology might include anti-social personality disorder or narcissistic personality disorder, to name two. Of course, these are hypotheses that need to be evaluated. Nothing toward a formulation has yet been presented.

In evaluating the first complaint of the individual, and for that matter in evaluating all complaints, the therapist should be guided by the behavioral analysis matrix (Table 3.1) (Turkat, 1979). This matrix shows the antecedents and consequences of problems, whether they are environmental, cognitive, autonomic, or motoric. Whether one specifies the problem and operationalizes it in terms of the behavioral analysis matrix at the beginning discussion of the problem, later discussion of the problem, or other points in the interview depends on too many variables for a general rule to be articulated. The only guiding principle is the overall premise of this approach: Do what you need to do in order to develop a useful formulation.

Multiple Problem Description

Rarely does a clinical case have only one presenting problem. When one is working with personality disorders, a whole menu of complaints and difficulties is presented. Thus, it is critical to develop an exhaustive list of all the problems of the patient. These should include not only

Table 3.1. The Behavior Analysis Matrix

	A (Antecedent)	B (Behavior)	C (Consequence)
C (Cognitive)	X	X	X
A (Autonomic)	X	X	X
M (Motor)	X	X	X
E (Environmental)	X		X

Note. From "Behavioral analysis of clinical cases," by V. Meyer and I.D. Turkat, 1979, *Journal of Behavioral Assessment, 1*, pp. 259–270. Copyright 1979 by Plenum Publishing Corporation. Reprinted by permission.

those difficulties that the patient can identify by himself or herself but also other problems that the patient may be experiencing that can be hypothesized by the clinician. Often, the therapist will continue to press the individual to make the list of problems as detailed as possible. In fact, this is typically done until the patient cannot specify any more. Naturally, this probing should not be done in an interrogating fashion but rather in a manner in which the patient feels comfortable. To accomplish this the therapist must develop an understanding of the individual and adapt to him or her. In other words, a standard approach, such as Rogerian reflection, is not indicated (Turkat & Alpher, 1983; Turkat & Brantley, 1981). Discussion of issues involving the relationship to the patient will be presented later on.

In specifying each problem, the therapist keeps the behavioral analysis matrix in mind and uses it accordingly. For certain problems, considerable time is spent operationalizing the patient's concerns. In some circumstances, this may not be necessary. Again, data and hypotheses dictate the sequence of events.

Hypothesis Generation

By the time the therapist has developed an exhaustive problem list, he or she should have a strong hypothesis about how these problems are related. If there is no hypothesis that accounts for all the patient's difficulties, the therapist must continue to search for useful information in this regard. In other words, new data must be generated with the hope that it will shed light on the matter. There are various ways to do this. For example, focusing on the primary concern of the patient and going through its history may prove helpful. Another tactic is to operationalize each problem in terms of the behavioral analysis matrix and then compare the various matrices in regard to a more "global behavioral analysis matrix." A third strategy involves interviewing a relevant, significant other (i.e., someone who has been identified as having important information regarding the patient's problem). A fourth avenue (not recommended for use in all cases) is to apply certain psychological tests such as the Minnesota Multiphasic Personality Inventory (MMPI; MMPI-2). Yet another way to collect data is to observe the patient in the situation in which he or she is having the most difficulty. Finally, in certain cases, it is most appropriate to refer the individual to someone else.

Etiology Inquiries

Etiology inquiries refer to the predisposing, precipitating, and main-taining factors of the patient's difficulties. A predisposing factor is any variable that might have made the patient vulnerable to developing the problems that he or she has indeed developed, given that the right conditions occurred at some point. Precipitating events are those specific triggers that appear to generate the problem immediately. Maintaining factors are those variables that perpetuate the patient's difficulties, once they have appeared.

Predisposing Factors.   The range of predisposing factors is considerable and the stage in the interview in which one goes about discovering them varies as well. In terms of some common predisposing factors, examination of the attributes of the patient's parents is usually quite helpful. Further, knowing the physical, social, cultural, academic, religious, interpersonal, medical, and legal background is also important. If we assume that the development of a personality disorder is a function of the interaction between genes and environment, the personality descriptions given by the patient of his or her mother and father can provide data that can be used to construct hypotheses about what the patient may or may not have learned (or acquired in other ways) from the parents. For example, assume the patient's father is described as being impulsive. Further, assume the patient has a difficult time controlling his or her own impulses. This tendency may be passed on biologically, learned by watching the impulsive parent struggle with similar difficulties, or perhaps be a function of brain injury following a car accident. The point is that there are many different routes by which a problem may emerge; these must be considered when searching for predisposing, triggering, or maintaining factors.

In the assessment of predisposing factors, the therapist may prefer first to develop hypotheses about the relationship among complaints and then ask, "What factors would I expect to see as predispositions if the hypothesized relationship among the complaints is true?" In this sense, he or she can then hypothesize the type of parents, parental upbringing, and experiences that should be in the history. If these do not emerge, the therapist must either assume the hypotheses are incorrect or that the data are not being presented accurately. In this sense, merely getting "background information," as so many clinicians are trained to do without a guiding, sensitive formulation in mind, is not only highly inefficient but may also waste a considerable amount of energy and money (Wolpe & Turkat, 1985).

Precipitating Variables.   As mentioned above, precipitating events are those factors that elicit a problem. The easiest way to examine triggering events is simply to ask the patient, "When was the first time this occurred?" or "How did this develop?" Most individuals will be able to pinpoint their own hypotheses about the origin of their difficulties and often these are accurate. However, it is extremely common for the patient's first response to be "I have no idea." When this occurs, it is important to press on, in an appropriate way, to obtain the patient's hypotheses. Even if the patient is wrong, that fact in itself is useful data, and how the patient has conceptualized his or her own developmental history should make sense in light of the emerging formulation of the patient's problem.

In examining the precipitating events, the therapist should become as operational as possible in the description. Again, the details should make sense in regard to the therapist's ideas about what the problems are, how they are related, and how they developed. If the details violate this viewpoint, the therapist should question the validity of something, whether it is his or her hypotheses or the accuracy of the information being presented.

Maintaining Factors.   Examination of the variables that perpetuate a disorder is critical in understanding the presenting case. The most useful approach is to follow the development of the problem chronologically from its origin to the present. In this manner, if the individual is pressed to specify each major significant change in the problem in regard to its worsening and improving, the events associated with these changes should make sense in terms of why the problems have continued. If they do not, the *therapist* has a problem that he or she must solve.

The Formulation

Once the therapist is able to relate the problems to each other and to specify the predisposing, triggering, and perpetuating variables, he or she is in a position to make some predictions about the patient's behavior in the future. At this stage, the criteria for developing a formulation have been met. It is this critical theory about the individual that will play such a vital role in the entire process of helping him or her to change in a constructive way.

Once the clinician has constructed a valid formulation, it is used to guide subsequent therapeutic interactions. The formulation should include not only relevant aspects of the specific plan of therapeutic actions but should also specify critical dimensions for the therapeutic relationship. For example, in cases in which the patient has a problem tolerating boredom, the therapist will need to act in a novel and stimulating manner to keep the client motivated during their interactions. However, as the patient becomes more skilled in controlling the intolerance of boredom during the active treatment plan, the nature of the therapeutic relationship would parallel this: the therapist would become increasingly less stimulating.

Once the formulation has been generated, it should be shared with the patient for comments. From an ethical standpoint, the patient certainly has the right to have access to the therapist's understanding of his or her dilemma, and presentation of that conceptualization should be integral to intervention efforts. I prefer to present the formulation not only to gauge the patient's reactions but also to make clear the reasons that particular intervention strategies will be adopted. My clinical experience has shown that the vast majority of individuals are relieved when they hear the clinician's formulation.

The following 14 points are often covered when presenting a formulation [from "The behavioral interview" by I.D. Turkat. In A.R. Ciminero, K.S. Calhoun, & H.E. Adams (Eds.) *Handbook of behavioral assessment* (2nd ed.) (pp. 109–149), 1986, New York: John Wiley & Sons. Copyright © 1986 by John Wiley & Sons. Reprinted by permission of John Wiley & Sons, Inc.]:

1. Informing the patient that the clinician's formulation of the problem will be presented and that the patient should comment on its accuracy.
2. Stating the presenting problems.
3. Explaining the general mechanism of the disorder.
4. Illustrating how this mechanism is causing all the presenting problems.
5. Explaining why these problems developed, using examples provided by the patient.
6. Emphasizing how these responses have been acquired.
7. Outlining the range of treatment options.
8. Discussing all the positive and negative consequences expected from each treatment option.
9. Predicting obstacles to successful intervention.
10. Stating whether the therapist can treat the patient, and if not, why not.
11. Asking the patient to comment on all that has been said.
12. Asking the patient what he or she believes would be the best option to follow.
13. Encouraging the patient to spend a week or so contemplating the formulation, its indications, and treatment options.
14. Answering any questions the patient asks.

In making the presentation, point 6 above is critical. Reviewing how the patient acquired the current difficulties permits the clinician to be able to state to the patient, "If I had the same history as you, I would have the same difficulties." This comment often provides considerable relief to the patient and helps the dyad become more cohesive (toward working to reach a goal, not as an end in itself).

CLINICAL EXPERIMENTATION

When the case formulation tripartite model was first presented (Meyer & Turkat, 1979), clinical experimentation was described as activity that "attempted to isolate the independent and dependent variables" involved in the client's difficulties. For example, two individuals presenting severe compulsive motor rituals involving hand washing and fears of contamination will differ in the precise stimuli and responses involved. Whereas in one case the clinician may find rituals involving use of a particular lotion, the other case may not use lotions at all in hand cleansing. Further, where one's fear of contamination leading to rituals may be triggered by touching toilets, the other case may involve the urge to ritualize in response to thoughts that have nothing to do with toilets.

As the case formulation model developed further, Turkat and Maisto (1985) expanded the clinical experimentation phase to attempt to verify the validity of the clinician's formulation of the patient's difficulties. In other words, clinical experimentation was intended not only to specify further the precise stimuli and responses (or independent and dependent variables) but also to subject the formulation to a test of its usefulness. In this sense, specific predictions derived from the formulation were evaluated in quasi-experimental fashion. For example, in the case of Ms. R, a histrionic personality disorder with a hypothesized empathy deficit (Turkat & Maisto, 1985), the patient engaged in certain quasi-experimental tasks to determine whether she would act in the predicted nonempathic manner under standardized conditions.

Currently I engage in clinical experimentation utilizing both the Meyer and Turkat (1979) strategy and the Turkat and Maisto (1985) strategy where appropriate. When the formulation is considered valid, further specifications of the precise independent and dependent variables will still need to be accomplished; hence, the Meyer and Turkat (1979) definition. In other cases, when a novel formulation is being presented, clinical experimentation aims to test its validity. In either case, *the critical issue is the question or hypothesis that is guiding the activity.* I seldom administer psychological tests prior to developing a formulation (see Carey, Flasher, Maisto, & Turkat, 1984), preferring a priori hypothesis generation. Thus, for example, if the patient was given the Symbol Digit Modalities Test (Smith, 1982) in clinical experimentation, certain predictions would have been made. If the patient's responses were not as predicted, the validity of the formulation would be questioned. However, in the undesired occurrence in which the therapist has attempted to construct the formulation, has been unable to do so, and has determined to give a psychological test such as the MMPI-2 as a means of collecting data to help develop a formulation, the activity would no longer be considered clinical experimentation. Thus, clinical experimentation is dependent on the hypothesis or question being asked and not merely on the activity that is occurring.

There are many difficulties in engaging in clinical experimentation. First, there are few clinical experiments that are easily administered for the purposes of everyday clinical practice. Second, norm-referenced basic assessment instruments are often insensitive to the types of independent and dependent variables of interest when one is utilizing the formulation-based approach of this text. Third, clinicians often do not have the luxuries of time, resources, and finances to engage in clinical experimentation. Finally, patients seeking immediate symptomatic relief would often find it objectionable to engage in a lengthy experimentation. The overriding difficulty with clinical experimentation is that the clinician is not in a position to engage in scientific activity with a patient that would allow a strong inference to be made (Platt, 1966). At best, the clinician is able to engage in a strategy of seeking converging evidence for the validity of the formulation. However, the strategy's implementation rarely enables the exclusion of other viable hypotheses. It should be obvious that when one is implementing clinical experimentation, one is not engaging in rigorous research. The clinician *should not be expected* to conduct rigorous research. Should evidence that supports the formulation be developed, clinicial experimentation can bolster the confidence of both clinician and patient in the theory that has been constructed to guide the therapeutic process (Turkat, 1988).

Not all cases require the clinical experimentation approach to obtain convergent validity evidence. When patients present problems for which established formulations and interventions are available, it makes little sense (either for the clinician or the patient) to engage in redundant testing. However, the common circumstance, particularly with the personality disorders, is that evidence regarding the formulation and modification of the presenting case is lacking in the scientific literature. In such circumstances, clinical experimentation is quite appropriate.

Given the tremendous range of variables that could be generated from the diverse nature of psychopathology presented by personality disorder cases as well as the infinite possibilities involved in formulations of those behavior problems, it is impossible at present to articulate very specific step-by-step guidelines for engaging in clinical experimentation. The notion is in its infancy and at the present time its success in everyday clinical practice depends on the ingenuity and skill of the particular clinician involved.

Ultimately, the usefulness of engaging in clinical experimentation will be determined by scientific evidence. Currently, there is no such evidence on the subject.

MODIFICATION METHODOLOGY

The development of a specific plan of action for managing difficulties presented by a particular client is highly dependent on the formulation of the case. Just because a patient may present, for example, an anxiety problem does not mean that he or she will undergo anxiety management training. Rather, the formulation of the patient's problems and the predictions that come from that formulation will determine the nature of the treatment plan.

The first step in developing the treatment plan is for the therapist to share the case formulation with the patient and for both to agree that they will operate on the assumption that it is valid. Direct implications can be specified; these will then be translated into *ideal treatment*. However, ideal treatment may not necessarily mean intervention that is practical. Sharing the formulation with the patient helps in the development of realistic expectations. Predicting obstacles to treatment is an important aspect of a useful formulation because the treatment plan should be engineered so as to maximize its likelihood of success. Having the patient understand the formulation can help him or her outline difficulties in implementing any particular treatment plan that perhaps the therapist was unable to predict.

The case formulation also determines the specific nature of the therapeutic interactions during the course of treatment. A standardized Rogerian approach of reflections is considered highly inappropriate, as is any standard approach to interacting with patients. In cases in which patients have a severe fear of rejection (as in the avoidant personality disorder), the therapist is often initially accepting; as the patient becomes more and more able to tolerate rejection through anxiety management training, the therapist becomes less accepting, paralleling the treatment program. Or, in dealing with individuals who are excessively orderly and logical at the expense of emotional reactivity (as in the obsessive compulsive personality disorder), the therapist may initially behave in a logical, systematic, orderly fashion; as treatment progresses successfully, the therapist becomes increasingly less orderly and more emotional in interactions with the patient. Again, the formulation of the case dictates the specific aspects of the therapeutic relationship. In this sense, a technological or standardized approach to dealing with psycho-pathology is quite incompatible with the approach presented in this text.

Intervention Sequencing

The formulation of the case should determine the order in which any range of problems or any intervention should be approached. For example, assume we are dealing with a paranoid personality disorder in which the hypothesized major problem tying together the various difficulties is a hypersensitivity to criticism (see Turkat, 1985). Assume further that the patient has poor social skills. The formulation of the case might specify that the patient would need to learn to control his or her anxiety to criticism before engaging in social skills training because he or she may be too anxious to be able to learn from the type of criticism that would be provided in social skills training. On the other hand, another patient who may also have anxiety in response to criticism and poor social skills may require social skills training first. In this particular case the formulation might be that the primary problem is the patient's social behavior and that the anxiety about criticism is secondary because the patient is engaging in behavior that invites criticism. While on the surface it appears that two cases may have the same problems, not only may the treatments differ, but they will differ based on the predictions of the formulation.

This aspect of devising the treatment plan and the specifics of intervention sequencing, based on the formulation, illustrates the dif-ference between formulation-based clinical activity and standardized behavioral therapy. Many behavioral therapists have proposed, when encountering patients with multiple problems, to start first with either the most "problematic" problem, the problem that is most likely to lead to a successful outcome or, in many cases, no specification. The implication of a formulation-based approach is that many of these options are often inadequate.

Treatment Implementation

The specifics of implementing any particular treatment procedure will vary depending on the indications of the formulation. It is particularly important for the therapist to keep in mind the predicted obstacles that should arise. Some of these will need to be shared with the patient so that he or she will understand what is occurring when the intervention appears not to be helping at any particular moment. In other cases, the therapist may decide not to share certain expected obstacles from fear of potentially sabotaging the outcome. It is difficult to set out rules that the clinician should follow in this regard. Again, it is the understanding of the case that influences this determination.

Treatment Evaluation

One of the most important developments in the last few decades is the advance that has occurred in single-case experimental design for evaluating treatment efficacy. The overwhelming majority of this literature is devoted to evaluating treatment effects rather than testing hypotheses about psychopathology, as in clinical experimentation (Turkat & Maisto, 1985). There are excellent volumes available outlining single-case methodology to which the reader is referred (Barlow & Hersen, 1984; Davidson & Costello, 1969; Hersen & Barlow, 1976).

Some individuals have argued in the literature that all patients should be completing dependent measures in a systematic manner throughout the course of treatment. Some have even suggested taking measures as frequently as daily. My viewpoint is different: the formulation of the case should determine the nature of evaluations that would be useful and likely to be utilized. Taking daily measures will rarely be accepted by the vast majority of patients; for many it would seem unnecessary to derive conclusions about whether they are improving. Simple pre- and posttests can often be quite useful. Further, in certain difficulties it is clear, just from everyday clinical observations of the patient, whether improvement has occurred; therefore, it makes little sense to force a more structured evaluation merely for the appearance of "being scientific." Each case is different and should be handled accordingly.

Session Frequency

There is no standard approach for scheduling a patient's therapy sessions. Rather, it is the formulation of the problem that determines the frequency and length of intervention interactions (Turkat, 1982). Some patients may need to be seen once every 2 weeks for 25 minutes whereas others may need to be hospitalized. Some cases may require three 45-minute sessions weekly at first, a frequency that will subsequently change as progress in treatment is made.

Other Interventions

In many cases, the formulation will specify needs for intervention that cannot be met by the clinician. If the patient requires medication and the clinician is not a physician, appropriate referral needs to be made. In many cases, additional support personnel such as a social worker, speech pathologist, occupational therapist, physical therapist, attorney, or financial counselor may be important. The clinician should not think that he or she must be able to do everything for everyone. There are many experts in other fields; that expertise should be tapped when it is necessary for the client's well-being.

Chapter 4
Illustration of the Psychological Approach

In this section, application of the presented psychological approach to personality disorder cases is illustrated. The first case example reveals how a formulation is constructed. The second case exemplifies one approach to the use of clinical experimentation with a particular personality disorder patient. The third example illustrates the construction and implementation of a treatment plan for an individual suffering from a type of personality pathology different from the first two characterological disordered case examples. Each of the illustrations in this chapter is one of the DSM-III-diagnosed personality disorders that have been presented elsewhere (Turkat & Maisto, 1985), providing further details for the interested reader.

CASE ONE: FORMULATION DEVELOPMENT ILLUSTRATION

The patient (Mr. E) was a 52-year-old Caucasian male who was self-referred. At the beginning of the initial interview, the patient stated that he sought professional help because his wife would no longer have sex with him. Mr. E said that he had been married for 22 years and that 4 years ago his wife had had a hysterectomy. Since that time his wife had refused to have sexual relations with him because she considered him to be unattractive, overweight, and boring. Ten presenting problems were identified as follows.

1. *Sexual problems.* Mr. E reported that before his wife's hysterectomy, they would have sexual intercourse every night. He reported that each night both experienced multiple orgasms. (These statements diminish confidence in the accuracy of the patient's self-reports.) As

previously noted, after the hysterectomy they reportedly stopped having sex. Further, the patient indicated that he had had no sexual interactions with any other individuals during this period, but that he currently masturbated "one to four times a week."

2. *Marital problems.* Mr. E said that his wife constantly criticized him. In particular, Mrs. E was reported as frequently reminding the patient that he was a failure in whatever he attempted. She also told Mr. E frequently that he was boring and unattractive.

3. *Depression.* The patient reported experiencing frequent bouts of depression. He often ruminated during these episodes about many topics that he found aversive. These are elaborated on below.

4. *Family problems.* Mr. E reported problems with his wife, three children, and mother. He said that his family was disturbed about his repeated ruminations and his discussions about the past 30 years (see problem 6) which they claimed considerably disrupted the family's life. Mr. E also told of several outbursts of violence with his children because of his preoccupation with the past.

5. *Job dissatisfaction.* Mr. E said that he was dissatisfied with his present position as a clerk in a sheriff's department. At the time of the initial interview, Mr. E had been employed in that position for 11 years. He reported considerable distress about being passed over for promotion several times. Further, he felt that he deserved a position of higher status.

6. *Ruminations about the past.* The patient reported spending much of the day thinking about the past and said that he was unable to stop. These thoughts primarily concerned failures in the many academic and employment settings that had marked his life. There did not seem to be any one episode that dominated his ruminations.

7. *Loneliness.* The patient initially reported that he had many friends. However, further discussion revealed that he actually had no close friends and had no social contacts outside of work. Mr. E initially referred to his co-workers as friends but later admitted that he did not spend any time outside of work socializing with them. Consequently, he felt lonely.

8. *Obesity.* Mr. E was approximately 35 pounds overweight at the time of the initial interview. He reported that he would eat more when he felt nervous, upset, or depressed.

9. *Smoking.* The patient reported excessive cigarette smoking, which also was correlated with his feelings of anxiety and depression.

10. *Muscle twitching.* Mr. E said that he often developed involuntary muscle twitching in the face. These episodes occurred exclusively when Mr. E was alone at night and when he was ruminating about his past.

History

The patient reported that he was an only child who was rather large and fat. He described his mother as a "bitchy, spoiled woman" whom he found extremely difficult to get along with because she often criticized him. Mr. E's father divorced the patient's mother and left the house when Mr. E was 3 years old. Mr. E did not see his father again until he was 18 years old. When the patient's father moved out of the home, his maternal grandfather moved in and assumed the father role. Mr. E described his grandfather as a successful judge and lawyer who was "loved by everyone who knew him." He also described his grandfather as the "perfect southern gentleman." Mr. E stated that he was reared in a strict religious home. Both his grandfather and mother were affiliated with a fundamentalist religious denomination and followed its doctrines strictly.

Mr. E's social history was characterized by isolation and loneliness, and he described his grandfather as his only good friend. Mr. E reported that as a child and later in life he had always been the target of others' criticisms. For example, one of his nicknames was "fatty meat." Furthermore, the patient said that during childhood he was often "smacked in the mouth" by the other children (despite his large size) for "no reason at all." When he would go home to his mother for comfort, she would reply, "Don't bother me, fend for yourself." Mr. E reported that he always tried to be nice to everyone so that they would like him but that it never seemed to work.

The patient did not do well academically. He said that after high school graduation he enrolled in and was expelled from eight different colleges and universities because of failing grades. He reported that while studying he felt extremely insecure and nervous, a condition that resulted in his inability to learn the material. He also reported feeling so anxious during exams that he could not concentrate. Nevertheless, he continued to consider the achievement of a strong educational background to be an important goal and aspired to earn a professional degree. Although Mr. E viewed his educational background as a series of failures, he liked to "impress" others by his "educational aspirations."

Mr. E related a similarly unstable job history. Over the past 20 years, the patient had been hired and fired from numerous jobs as a salesman, dishwasher, taxi driver, and worker in a paint warehouse and drugstore chain.

The patient's sexual history revealed that he had had no sexual encounters other than with his wife. As an adolescent, and in his early 20s, he reported having had many offers for sexual activity but that he had avoided them because of his religious beliefs and his fear of being sexually inadequate. He indicated that at times he felt that his penis was too small and that he feared others thought he might be homosexual (although he denied this). In fact, the patient reported that certain females had accused him of being homosexual because he had refused to have sex with them. Mr. E had dated his current wife only one time before he married her. The patient had not seen his wife for some time after the first date until one day she approached Mr. E and asked him to "run off and get married." Mr. E felt that he would never have an opportunity to marry anyone so he accepted the offer.

At the initial interview the patient reported spending a considerable amount of time ruminating about his past. He continuously thought in detail about his failures in educational pursuits. Mr. E fluctuated between thinking that everyone was against him and thinking that perhaps he was a genius. He felt that being a genius might have made it impossible for him to learn in the typical academic environment. The patient also thought frequently about his grandfather. While he felt that his grandfather was "special" and was grateful that his grandfather "took him under his wing," Mr. E felt angry toward his grandfather for creating such high standards for him to meet. In this regard the patient spent much of his time thinking about his special skills as a "perfect southern gentleman," skills like those of his grandfather. However, he also thought about times when people made critical comments about southerners in general; these remarks led Mr. E to hate being a southerner. Finally, the patient's preoccupation with the past and his many failures led him to explain, even to acquaintances, the circumstances surrounding these episodes so that his goals or aspirations would not be misunderstood. As an example, Mr. E reported that while waiting to pay for an item at a drugstore, he began explaining to another person whom he had just met in line much of his history and how he had been "screwed over."

Diagnosis

The presenting problems of this patient suggested a primary DSM-III diagnosis of paranoid personality disorder. Specifically, he was always on guard for others' misunderstandings of him and attempted to avoid any possible blame by explaining to others why circumstances were against him. He tended to be easily slighted, exaggerated the severity of his mistakes, and was unable to relax. Finally, he tried to present an image of rationality and objectivity and he lacked a true sense of humor.

Formulation

The patient was an only child who had physical characteristics that made him a target of social criticism. His mother appeared to be cold, and she criticized the patient frequently. She did not provide any comfort or reassurance when the patient was humiliated or hurt by others, instead suggesting that he should learn to fend for himself. Since the father left the home when Mr. E was only 3 years old, it appeared that the grandfather filled the father role. In this regard the patient was presented with a model of a "perfect southern gentleman." The grandfather was reportedly "loved and admired" by everyone, and the patient viewed him with considerable respect. The grandfather also was seen as "special" and treated the patient in a similar manner by "taking him under his wing." It appeared that, given the high standards of performance modeled by the grandfather, combined with the criticism from the patient's peers and his mother and elicited by his physical characteristics, he developed appropriate self-evaluations of inadequacy and insecurity and a fear of failure. The patient felt that he never could live up to the standards modeled by his grandfather. Nevertheless, he tried to become like his grandfather by pursuing academic training to become a professional. Unfortunately, he failed repeatedly.

As a function of this history, it was hypothesized that the patient had developed a hypersensitivity to others' evaluations of him. This condition led to social isolation and little opportunity to develop good social skills. As a result, a cycle was created in which the patient was afraid of others' opinions, attempted to make a good impression, but did so in such a way as to invite criticism, which caused even further isolation. During this isolation the patient was preoccupied with his failures and viewed himself as inadequate and persecuted. The variety and frequency of his thinking about his failures, combined with frequent actual failure experiences, led Mr. E to rationalize his predicament by viewing himself at first with persecution and later with grandeur.

It appeared that the patient's hypersensitivity to others' evaluations was the general mechanism accounting for his problems. The patient was so concerned about others' evaluations that he frequently tried to ensure that others did not "misunderstand him" by going over his history and his failures, pointing out how circumstances were set against him. Obviously, this attitude made him an undesirable social partner, a "boring" and irritating marital partner, and in combination with his large frame and obesity, an unattractive sexual partner, all of which led to further social isolation. As a result, the patient felt lonely and depressed. While alone, he ruminated about his past to the extent that his face would become so tight with muscle tension that he would start twitching. When his anxiety increased, he would increase his eating and smoking. Finally, he was dissatisfied with his present job because it reminded him that he could never reach his desired level of aspiration.

With this conceptualization in mind, several predictions can be made about the patient's behavior in response to future stimulus conditions. A few of these predictions are listed below.

First, the patient should demonstrate increased subjective anxiety and autonomic arousal to criticisms that are inappropriate in degree when compared with others (be they normal or disordered) who do not have the hypothesized hypersensitivity to evaluation.

Second, if the patient's hypersensitivity to criticism is not modified, the patient's symptomatic complaints (e.g., facial twitching, depression) will continue.

Third, if the patient reduces his hypersensitivity to criticism and subsequent changes in other symptoms occur, his marital situation might change (e.g., it may worsen).

Fourth, in learning how to overcome being sensitive to criticism, the patient will initially be autonomically aroused, fearing criticism for his performance in learning the new skill.

The reader should now be able to appreciate the range of predictions made possible by developing a formulation of this kind and the relevance of the predictions for treatment planning and implementation.

CASE TWO: CLINICAL EXPERIMENTATION ILLUSTRATION

This illustration is of a 22-year-old Caucasian female (Ms. R) who presented 13 behavioral problems (e.g., nonadherence to a medically necessary diet, ease of boredom, shallow social relations) that were conceptualized as the result of an impulse control deficit. She received a DSM-III diagnosis of narcissistic personality disorder (Turkat & Maisto, 1985). In testing the hypothesis of an impulse control deficit, a convergent evidence approach was used. Four specific hypotheses were evaluated.

Hypothesis 1

It was predicted that the patient would choose an immediate, smaller reinforcement over a delayed, larger reinforcement for performance on a boring task.

Test of Hypothesis 1.   During the first testing session, Ms. R was given a work task that involved crossing out certain letters of the alphabet on a typewritten sheet. She was given two choices: (a) crossing out all the o's and e's that appeared in the text, with an immediate payment of 10 cents for each line correctly crossed out, or (b) crossing out all the i's and a's that appeared, for which she was to receive 20 cents for each correct line one month after the session. The patient assumed that she could perform both options simultaneously, despite the instructions to choose only one. Accordingly, over the 10-minute period, she crossed out all the specified o's, e's, i's, and a's on 17 lines, an action that netted $1.70 immediately and $3.40 to be reimbursed later. To correct the misunderstanding in instructions, the patient was retested in Session 2 when the work task was repeated with two minor changes. First, she was forced to make a choice between option (a), immediate reinforcement (one reinforcer), and option (b), delayed reinforcement (three reinforcers). Second, instead of money, cigarettes were used as reinforcement because they cost less and were identified as strong reinforcers to the patient. A second trial of the work task involved a choice between receiving one cigarette for each line immediately or a later reinforcement of five cigarettes per line.

On the first trial the patient chose the immediate reinforcement (one cigarette) over the delayed reinforcement (three cigarettes at the end of the month) as predicted. On the second trial Ms. R chose delayed reinforcement (five cigarettes a line) over the immediate reinforcement of one cigarette. On the first trial she earned 35 cigarettes for 35 lines, and on the second trial she earned 185 cigarettes for 35 lines. Therefore, Ms. R performed as predicted on the first trial, when she chose an immediate reinforcement that was one third the value of the delayed reinforcement. On the second trial she chose the delayed reinforcement because, she said, "I already had earned enough cigarettes for today."

In order to replicate the original finding without confounding previous earnings, the experiment was repeated in Session 3. In this experiment a choice to cross out o's and e's resulted in immediate payment of one cigarette. In contrast, a choice of crossing out a's and i's resulted in payment of five cigarettes a line at the end of the month. As predicted, Ms. R chose immediate reinforcement even though the delayed reinforcement paid off at five times the rate of immediate reinforcement. Accordingly, it was concluded that Hypothesis 1 was supported.

Hypothesis 2

It was predicted that the patient would eat more desirable food following a period of no immediate social reinforcement compared to the amount eaten after immediate social reinforcement was provided.

Test of Hypothesis 2. During the first testing session, the patient was asked to list her favorite brands of snack food such as crackers, cookies, and pretzels. During Session 2, she was given a monotonous, boring task to work on for 20 minutes. The task consisted of completing a series of Symbol Digit Modalities Test (Smith, 1982) sheets. In this session Ms. R was given no encouragement and was simply instructed to complete the task as quickly as she could. She remained alone in the room while completing the task. After 20 minutes, she was told that a "taste test" (cf. Schachter & Rodin, 1974) would be conducted that had no apparent connection to the digit test. The experimenters placed three plates of crackers before the subject and read the following instructions to her:

> We have three types of crackers we would like you to taste. You are to rate each of them on the characteristics on this sheet (an adjective checklist including "tasty," "salty," etc.). Eat as few or as many as you want—the only requirement is that you taste each one at least once. You will have 15 minutes to do this.

After the taste test was completed, the crackers were removed to another room and the quantity and weight of crackers consumed was determined. In Session 3, the patient was given the same monotonous task to do for 20 minutes. However, every 5 minutes the experimenter entered the room and encouraged her by saying that she was doing well or that she was working quickly. At the end of 20 minutes, three plates of crackers (same quantity and quality as in the first test but different brands) were brought in, and Ms. R was again asked to taste and rate three types of crackers. After 15 minutes, the crackers were removed, and the quantity and weight of the crackers consumed was recorded.

During the no reinforcement condition (i.e., the first exposure), the patient ate a total of 42 grams of crackers. During the attention condition (i.e., experimenter in the room attending to her), Ms. R ate only 20 grams of crackers. Thus, as predicted, Ms. R ate more than twice the amount of crackers after the *no attention* condition, compared with the *attention* condition. Both of the taste test sessions were run at 2:00 p.m. exactly 1 week apart. Ms. R arrived at each session without having eaten for 2 hours.

Hypothesis 3

It was predicted that the patient would score in the upper percentiles of the Sensation Seeking Scale (Zuckerman, 1979).

Test of Hypothesis 3. In order to test Hypothesis 3, the patient completed the Sensation Seeking Scale, Form V, in Session 2. The patient achieved a total score of 27, which was at the 95th percentile for females in a normative sample of undergraduates enrolled in an introductory psychology course (Zuckerman, 1979). Thus, Hypothesis 3 was supported.

Hypothesis 4

It was predicted that the patient would appear to be more impulsive compared to other individuals.

Test of Hypothesis 4. For this hypothesis to be tested, the patient completed the MMPI during Session 2. The results indicated a 4–7–9 profile. As described by Lachar (1980), individuals with a 4–7 MMPI configuration demonstrate "excessive insensitivity . . . these persons may act with little control or forethought, violating social and legal restrictions and trampling on feelings of others needlessly . . . excessive alcohol indulgence or stepping out/promiscuity" (p. 84).

Individuals with a 4–9 configuration are described in Lachar (1980) as

> always associated with some form of acting out behavior. The individual exhibits an enduring tendency to get into trouble with his environment . . . arousal seeking and inordinate need for excitement and stimulation . . . impulsive and irresponsible . . . untrustworthy, shallow and superficial in their relationships to others. They typically have easy morals; they are selfish and pleasure-seeking. Many temporarily create a favorable impression because they are internally comfortable and free from inhibiting anxiety, worry and guilt but are actually quite deficient in their role-taking ability. Their judgment is notably poor and they do not seem to learn from past experiences. They lack the ability to postpone gratification of their desires and therefore have difficulty in any enterprise requiring sustained effort (p. 88).

Finally, a 7–9 configuration is described in Lachar (1980) as indicative of "(a) heightened energy level . . . patients often experience periods of impulsivity. . . . This patient may be somewhat self-centered and immature" (p. 133). Accordingly, Hypothesis 4 was supported.

The results of these experiments and controlled observations provide converging validity for the behavioral formulation of a deficit in impulse control, as each specific prediction was supported by the data. As hypothesized, the patient preferred immediate reinforcement over a delayed reinforcement of substantially higher value, she ate more food after receiving no attention compared with after receiving social attention, and her scores, compared with standardized measures, indicated that she was excessively impulsive and sensation seeking.

CASE 3: MODIFICATION
METHODOLOGY ILLUSTRATION

The case of a DSM-III-diagnosed dependent personality disorder (Mrs. S) is presented to illustrate the approach to developing and implementing a modification methodology.

This patient was a 48-year-old Caucasian woman whose 13-year-old daughter had recently been diagnosed as having insulin-dependent diabetes mellitus. The patient began to experience sleep difficulty; anxiety about her daughter, others, supermarkets, and reading materials; and depressive feelings. Initially the case could not be formulated according to the Meyer and Turkat (1979) criteria. However, the patient requested symptomatic behavioral treatment over the option of referral. Symptomatic treatment was thus initiated. It appeared to succeed. It is interesting that at the first increase in interim length between therapy sessions, the patient relapsed completely. A reanalysis of the case at this time enabled the therapist to develop a formulation that included the primary hypothesis of a hypersensitivity to independent decision making. This formulation was subsequently evaluated in clinical experimentation and the results led to its acceptance as valid. Accordingly, a modification methodology was devised, based on the hypothesized hypersensitivity to independent decision making.

Before the intervention program is reviewed, the reader needs to be made aware of the nature of the symptomatic treatment provided early in the case. Symptomatic treatment involved the following: (a) progressive muscular relaxation training; (b) development of a hierarchy (in this case, 15 items) of (imaginal and in vivo) diabetes-related anxiety-producing stimuli; (c) instruction in substituting adaptive cognitions (e.g., "There's nothing I can do about my daughter's condition, so it makes no sense to get upset about it") for anxiety-arousing ones; and (d) practice in (bidirectional) anxiety management (see Meyer & Reich, 1978; Turkat & Kuczmierczyk, 1980; and chapter 5).

Throughout treatment, Mrs. S worked diligently at learning anxiety-management skills. She was seen weekly for 4 months.

Following clinical experimentation and acceptance of a formulation, the latter was presented to and accepted by the patient. A new treatment procedure was devised that capitalized on the skills the patient had learned during the previous months of therapy. This treatment approach had several features. First, a 2-week interval for therapy sessions was maintained so as not to encourage the patient's dependence on the therapist. Second, practice of anxiety-management skills was emphasized. Further, a new hierarchy was developed. The new items included situations in which the patient had little experience and few guidelines for her behavior and required her to make decisions without the support and advice of others. With the assistance of the therapist, the patient developed a 16-item hierarchy. Examples of items in this hierarchy are planning supper with only the food in the refrigerator, seeking support from her husband when she felt ill but when he did not provide it, and interacting with people who asked about her daughter's condition when she was unsure of what to say. At this time the patient was also asked to perform daily self-ratings on the hierarchy items (which appeared on a standard checklist) using a score of 1 to 6 on which 1 represented *not anxious* and 6 represented *most anxious*. The patient's self-ratings were gathered for a 3-week baseline period, during the 2 months of treatment, and at follow-up periods of 2 weeks, 1 month, 4 months, and 11 months.

The patient's response to treatment was assessed primarily by daily self-monitoring of anxiety related to independent decision making. These data were analyzed across the three phases of therapy following the revised formulation (baseline, treatment, and follow-up), and the results indicated significant improvement. Anecdotal evidence revealed that the patient was subsequently able to manage independent decision-making situations that were not included in the treatment hierarchy. Further, the patient reported that she no longer experienced the anxiety, avoidance, and depression symptoms she initially experienced. These gains were maintained at an 11-month follow-up.

ILLUSTRATIONS CONSIDERED

In reviewing the cases of a paranoid personality disorder, a narcissistic personality disorder, and a dependent personality disorder, the reader should appreciate the dependence of the clinician on the formulation of the case. It is the formulation that determines the nature of clinical experimentation and modification methodology adaptions. This was readily illustrated with the case of Mrs. S. Without a formulation, Mrs. S was initially treated symptomatically, a course that led to a short-term improvement, then relapse. With a formulation, the validity of the clinician's ideas were evaluated objectively. With a formulation assumed to be valid, the clinician devised a treatment program that led to lasting improvement.

The next section of the book provides a review of my clinical experience in using the tripartite psychological model with DSM-III-R personality disorder cases. In particular, the emphasis is on providing clinically useful information. It must be noted that the clinical ideas to be presented are just that: ideas. While a particular framework for approaching clinical cases has helped to generate these ideas, there is no scientific evidence (to my knowledge) to support or refute them at present. It is hoped that the reader will find some useful notions for his or her own clinical and/or research practice in the following pages.

Part II

Clinical Experience with DSM-III-R
Personality Disorders

Chapter 5
Cluster A Personality Disorders

In 1987, the APA published a revised edition of the DSM-III, referred to as DSM-III-R (APA, 1987). According to Spitzer and Williams (1987), the chairperson of the work group to revise DSM-III and the text editor, respectively, thousands of scientific and clinical papers were written about the DSM-III during the 1980s. These manuscripts revealed significant benefit from and problems with the 1980 publication. Because of the problems identified, a decision was made to revise the DSM-III. Why the new edition was labeled DSM-III-R as opposed to DSM-IV is unclear. Although the timetable for DSM-IV projected its publication in the last decade of the 20th century, this is not a satisfactory explanation for the chosen label—DSM-III-R. In any event, the new version of psychiatric nosologic criteria was distributed in final form in 1987 and the implications for the personality disorders are briefly described below.

Organizationally, the DSM-III-R retains all of the DSM-III personality disorder categories except for the one titled "atypical, mixed, and other" which is now labeled "personality disorder not otherwise specified." Each of the personality disorders is placed into one of three clusters. Cluster A includes the paranoid personality disorder, the schizoid personality disorder, and the schizotypal personality disorder. This cluster is described as "the odd cluster" because such cases presumably present as being eccentric or weird.

Before the specifics of the Cluster A personality disorders are examined, the reader should note that the specific criteria for each personality disorder have been changed somewhat from those in the DSM-III. This change presents a variety of difficulties.

First, after the DSM-III was published in 1980, many scientists began research projects that attempted to utilize the new criteria. Several years are required to set up new diagnostic and assessment protocols for a clinical research project, run the experiment, analyze the results, write them up for publication, complete peer review, and then publish the findings. Because the diagnostic criteria were changed in such a short time period, many investigators were left with data that had been collected on DSM-III rather than DSM-III-R criteria, seriously impairing the utility of the data. Second, and most important, the changes in personality disorder criteria from the DSM-III to DSM-III-R have little to do with scientific evidence. (Readers should make their own decisions on this issue. It is suggested that they review for example, Widiger, Frances, Spitzer, and Williams, 1988.) Recent research suggests that the DSM-III-R personality disorder descriptions result in *increased* overlap among the categories, creating significant problems for researchers (Morey, 1988) and clinicians (Blashfield & Breen, 1989). In this sense, one of the major purposes for creating the DSM-III was not achieved in changing the personality pathology criteria for DSM-III-R.

Finally, clinicians require considerable time to learn to apply a new diagnostic system to their clinical practice. For this reason, they are less likely to adhere rigorously to rapid changes in diagnostic systems for scientific and communication purposes.

PARANOID PERSONALITY DISORDER

Perhaps the least researched type of personality disorder in the DSM-III-R is the paranoid personality disorder (Turkat, 1985). It is also the one that most clinicians consider untreatable according to the literature. Millon (1981) notes that "the prospects for the paranoid are poor. Therapeutic work with paranoids is a touchy proposition at best. Few come willingly to treatment" (pp. 397–398).

Clinically, it is understandable that suspicious, guarded, and distrustful individuals do not respond well to treatment. It has been shown that such individuals have been difficult to engage as research participants in scientific enterprises (Thompson-Pope & Turkat, 1989; Turkat & Banks, 1987). Nevertheless, there is no scientific evidence available today to demonstrate whether such cases can be treated successfully. The DSM-III-R criteria for paranoid personality disorder are presented in Table 5.1.

Interviewing the Patient

The patient with paranoid personality disorder does not complain about being paranoid, nor state that he or she is reading "hidden,

Table 5.1. DSM-III-R Criteria for Paranoid Personality Disorder

A. A pervasive and unwarranted tendency, beginning by early adulthood and present in a variety of contexts, to interpret the actions of people as deliberately demeaning or threatening, as indicated by at least four of the following:
 1. Expects, without sufficient basis, to be exploited or harmed by others
 2. Questions, without justification, the loyalty or trustworthiness of associates
 3. Reads hidden demeaning or threatening meanings into benign remarks or events, for example, suspects that a neighbor put out trash early to annoy him
 4. Bears grudges or is unforgiving of insults or slights
 5. Is reluctant to confide in others because of unwarranted fear that information will be used against him or her
 6. Is easily slighted and quick to react with anger or to counterattack
 7. Questions, without justification, fidelity of spouse or sexual partner
B. Occurrence not exclusively during the course of schizophrenia or a delusional disorder

Note: From American Psychiatric Association: *Diagnostic and statistical manual of mental disorders, third edition, revised.* Washington, DC, American Psychiatric Association, 1987. Reprinted with permission.

demeaning or threatening meanings into benign remarks or events" (APA, 1987). Such patients typically present initially with problems that reflect hostile and/or adversarial relationships with others. For example, one presented as wanting to learn how to be assertive. Another complained about being passed up for promotion at work. Yet another presented initially as being unable to relax. If clinicians took these complaints only at face value (as many therapists do) they would embark on treatment strategies matched to these complaints. They would also miss important aspects of the clinical phenomena being presented. If we ask "*Why* is this person having these problems"? we then begin to piece together an understanding. The patient seeking assertiveness training does so because he feels that everyone is "picking on him." To teach him to be assertive not only might miss the more important target of why he feels that he is being attacked, but also might backfire. The case of the individual being passed up for promotion would require considerable evaluation of what she is doing, or not doing, to prevent promotion. Such an examination requires openness to scrutiny, an attitude that is often difficult for the paranoid personality. To apply any behavioral treatment without first understanding what the problem is would be foolish and potentially hazardous. In the case of the person who reports being unable to relax, the therapist would be ill advised to begin applying progressive muscular relaxation without first asking, "Why is this person unable to relax?" Perhaps the patient has antagonized many significant others, creating significant hostility from them. If so, a different treatment would be required. The point is that merely taking statements at face value and acting upon them as if they are true can often lead the interviewer to miss a diagnosis of paranoid personality disorder.

To assess a case successfully, one should be suspicious of what the suspicious person is presenting. However, given that such patients are hypersensitive to threat, acting in a suspicious manner would only increase the patient's defensiveness. Thus, I recommend engaging in what has been termed "stepwise questioning" when interviewing such cases. With this questioning method, as described elsewhere (cf. Turkat, 1985; Turkat & Maisto, 1985), the interviewer appears supportive and understanding while progressively increasing the threatening nature of the questions. An example is presented in Table 5.2.

At the same time, although interrogating the patient would be an inappropriate approach for paranoid personality disorder, appearing too understanding would also arouse the patient's suspicions. An accepting but matter-of-fact approach often proves to be most useful.

Paranoid personality cases frequently present significant clues to the appropriate diagnosis early in the interview. It is my experience that in a good percentage of cases they spend either an inordinate amount of time reviewing the clinic's consent forms and often wish to discuss them before agreeing to be interviewed. Similarly, questions about whether the interview will be recorded or who has access to files are important clues. In most of these kinds of cases, there is something "different" about the patients. Some may be quite socially inept; others may be strikingly ugly; some may be alarmingly narrow in perspective. Attributes that make the individual stand out in a subtle way are often good tip-offs.

There is no common formulation of any particular case that can be rigidly applied across the board. Each patient presents a unique situation and history. There are, however, some general difficulties that seem to account for a significant range of paranoid personality pathology in a variety of such cases. One such viewpoint has been presented (Turkat, 1985). In the evaluative-uniqueness view, patients are trained early to be frightened at what other people think of them; often they have a unique

Table 5.2. An Example of Stepwise Questioning

Have you ever noticed that someone seemed to be giving you a hard time?
When that happened, did it seem as if this person were doing so deliberately?
Have you ever felt as if you were being picked on?
Even though this may sound strange, did it ever seem as though the other person may have been angry or maybe even jealous of you in some way?
Sometimes I interact with someone who seems jealous of me; have you experienced this?
What things might they be jealous of?
You know, sometimes, I feel that I have certain skills that people I interact with don't; how about you?
What special skills or talents do you have that others may be jealous of?
I know this may sound weird, but have you ever felt that you had any special powers?

---

attribute about which they are hypersensitive. One patient may view herself as being brighter than others. She may have been told this very early on and treated specially throughout her school years. In such cases, teaching the individual to become less sensitive to others' opinions and to use more appropriate social behaviors is indicated. The validity of the evaluative-uniqueness viewpoint has yet to be supported scientifically.

Clinical Experimentation

In many paranoid personality disorder cases, a theme that runs across the various presenting problems is often a hypersensivity to criticism. Because such hypersensitivity is so common, the clinician may wish to assess the validity of this notion in a particular patient. An appropriate illustration can be found in Turkat and Maisto (1985). Here, an individual diagnosed with paranoid personality disorder was viewed as having a hypersensitivity to criticism, which accounted for his difficulties. An experiment was devised in which the patient (Mr. E, see chapter 4) was exposed to criticisms and noncriticisms while being monitored for electromyographic (EMG) activity in the masseter muscle. The choice of dependent variable in this case was dictated by the patient's report of occasional twitching in this area when he was anxious. The independent variables were chosen in the following manner. First, explicit criticisms such as "being told by the therapist that you had made serious errors in the past," were presented. Implicit criticisms unique to that individual were also presented. An example of an implied criticism included having the patient look at a picture of General Lee surrendering to General Grant in the Civil War. In this particular case, because the patient was hypersensitive to remarks about southerners (as he viewed himself as "the perfect southern gentleman"), it was postulated that he would react with anxiety to a portrayal of the defeat of the south, a reaction that other individuals would not have. Explicit and implicit criticisms were counterbalanced with neutral stimuli in an A–B–A–B–A design.

The results of this experiment showed that the patient was hypersensitive to explicit and implicit criticisms in comparison to neutral scenes; explicit and implicit criticisms did not differ from each other. Thus, in this particular case, the hypothesized mechanism of disorder was supported.

It should be noted that not all clinicians have access to polygraph equipment and there are some useful norm-referenced tests that one can utilize with paranoid personality disorder cases to test hypotheses. The

Fear of Negative Evaluation Scale (Watson & Friend, 1969) can be useful. Further, the Speilberger Anger Expression Scale (STAXI) developed by Speilberger (1988) can be used as a dependent variable when the patient is asked to engage in situations that are threatening versus those that are not. Even more simply, just using a rating scale of 0 to 10 while manipulating critical stimuli can prove quite useful. The more dependent one is on the patient's self-report, however, the less confidence one has in the accuracy of the data (see Ciminero, Calhoun, & Adams, 1986).

Modification Methodology

There is no common set of formulations for paranoid personality disorder, nor is there any common set of intervention methods. However, many cases seem to benefit from two primary treatment approaches. First, in indicated cases, decreasing the patient's sensitivity to criticism often proves beneficial. Second, social skills training can sometimes be quite helpful.

Decreasing Sensitivity to Criticism. In regard to decreasing sensitivity to criticism, I have found bidirectional anxiety management (Meyer & Reich, 1978; Turkat & Kuczmierczyk, 1980) to be useful. The approach has several aspects. First, some type of antianxiety response is taught; this may involve muscular relaxation or some type of cognitive modification. Second, a biofeedback monitor that appears to have a good relationship between stimuli presented (which the patient has previously identified as anxiety generating) and physiologic arousal is used. These indicators may be galvanic skin response (GSR), EMG response, or other physiologic indicators. Third, a hierarchy of anxiety-provoking criticisms is generated. Then the patient is taught to bring on his or her anxiety. Once the anxiety is generated, instructions are provided to decrease it through the methods that have been taught previously (i.e., by applying the competing responses along with physiological feedback). In vivo hierarchical items are used as often as possible. As anxiety-managment skills progress, the physiological equipment is phased out of the treatment.

Some guidelines for noting treatment progress are available. First, low-level items on the hierarchy are typically self-generated (e.g., imaginal). As the patient begins to demonstrate control of the anxiety response, he or she will find it increasingly more difficult to self-generate anxiety. The amount of time that it takes the individual to decrease the anxiety once it has been elevated should be shorter. Thus, a simple reaction-time measure during practice with hierarchy items provides a relatively objective indicant of progress. Use of the feedback monitor should demonstrate control of the autonomic response to both therapist and patient. Finally, progression up the hierarchy is a useful indicant of treatment progress.

Modification of Social Behavior. In the modification of social behavior, there seem to be four key areas to evaluate. As proposed by Henry Adams, these include social attention, information processing, response emission, and feedback (Turkat & Maisto, 1985).

In regard to *social attention,* it is critical to determine whether the individual with paranoid personality disorder is in fact attending to the full range of appropriate stimuli. The therapist can assess this easily not only by reviewing important social interactions of the individual but also by having him or her view videotapes of others interacting or even watch segments of soap operas with the therapist present. The clinician then critically assesses how well the patient is responding to appropriate cues. If the patient is not identifying pertinent cues, the therapist can teach the patient how to do so by reviewing the situations exhaustively and repetitively, and explaining what the therapist is looking for that perhaps the patient is not.

In regard to *information processing,* the way in which the patient interprets social information is most important. As noted by research on paranoid personalities (Thompson-Pope & Turkat, 1988), such individuals have unique responses to ambiguous stimuli. Teaching these patients how to interpret social cues correctly is often an important component of social skills training. This training can often be accomplished with role playing, videotaped feedback, and instruction. In doing videotaped feedback and instruction, it is advisable to keep the interactions and/or stimuli presented very short in nature and to give immediate feedback by having the patient view himself or herself repeatedly while being taught to be self-critical and hence self-correcting. Initial sessions are taped; these are shown at a later date to reveal progress to both patient and therapist.

Response emission refers to the full range of executed social behaviors including one's physical appearance. In certain cases, the patient's tone of voice needs to be changed. In other cases, the individual must be taught to walk in a different way. In yet other cases, having the hair styled, learning to match colors in clothing, and adopting appropriate personal hygiene practices (e.g., choice of cologne) may be indicated for the patient.

Finally, it is critical that the patient be able to utilize the consequences of his or her social behavior appropriately. One of the major problems of individuals with untreated paranoid personality disorder is that they are so afraid of others' criticisms that they do not profit from negative *feedback.* However, negative feedback can be useful information and the patient needs to learn to use it constructively. Further, with improvement in social behavior, positive consequences should accrue to the patient. It is not uncommon for someone whose physical appearance dramatically improves to notice a change in others' reactions to him or her. Research has documented that perceptions of social behavior in the same individual can vary merely as a function of physical attractiveness (e.g., Guise, Pollans, & Turkat, 1982); therefore, clinical correlation should not be too surprising.

As the reader may surmise, although the majority of clinicians who have written about treatment of paranoid personality disorder cases suggest that it is untreatable, I believe that many such cases can in fact be treated successfully. This view has recently been endorsed by the APA Task Force on Treatments of Psychiatric Disorders (APA, 1989). However, scientific evidence needs to be generated.

SCHIZOID PERSONALITY DISORDER

The schizoid personality disorder has appeared throughout the APA's attempts at devising psychiatric nosologies. Its most recent formulation in the DSM-III-R is presented in Table 5.3.

The disorder is characterized primarily by lack of genuine affect in relating to others. Whereas the avoidant personality's reduced social involvement may be due to a fear of rejection, the schizoid personality simply does not care. It is interesting that research on the DSM-III schizoid personality disorder has revealed that it is infrequently diag-

Table 5.3.   DSM-III-R Criteria for Schizoid Personality Disorder

---

A. A pervasive pattern of indifference to social relationships and a restricted range of emotional experience and expression, beginning by early adulthood and present in a variety of contexts, as indicated by at least four of the following:
   1. Neither desires nor enjoys close relationships, including being part of a family
   2. Almost always chooses solitary activities
   3. Rarely, if ever, claims or appears to experience strong emotions, such as anger and joy
   4. Indicates little if any desire to have sexual experiences with another person (age being taken into account)
   5. Is indifferent to the praise and criticism of others
   6. Has no close friends or confidants (or only one) other than first-degree relatives
   7. Displays constricted affect, for example, is aloof, cold, rarely reciprocates gestures or facial expressions, such as smiles or nods
B. Occurrence not exclusively during the course of schizophrenia or a delusional disorder

---

Note: From American Psychiatric Association: *Diagnostic and statistical manual of mental disorders, third edition, revised.* Washington, DC, American Psychiatric Association, 1987. Reprinted with permission.

nosed clinically (cf. Widiger et al., 1988). The following discussion of the schizoid personality disorder focuses on the "true" schizoid: one who is indifferent to others.

Interviewing the Patient

Consistent with research findings (Widiger et al., 1988), it is my experience that few cases of schizoid personality disorder present clinically. When they do, the patient is often not the one who has initiated clinical contact. The more typical scenario is for someone else who is concerned about the patient to seek professional attention. Given the lifelong pattern of schizoid functioning that is assumed when a schizoid personality disorder diagnosis is warranted, the critical question is this: "What has transpired recently that should lead a significant other to prompt the schizoid personality to seek treatment at this time?" Generally, I have found that there will be one of two event sequences, which are not necessarily mutually exclusive.

In the first sequence, some event occurs that now interferes with the schizoid personality's ability to adhere to the earlier set patterns of social aloneness. For example, a physical disability arises, which precludes continuance of the socially distant daily routine.

The second pathway to professional attention may appear when the impact of the schizoid personality's functioning on a significant other changes to the detriment of the latter. In one case the schizoid personality gave up certain responsibilities, which increased the burden on the significant other who had historically compensated for the patient's social reclusiveness.

Regardless of how the patient with schizoid personality disorder arrives at the clinician's office, certain behavioral characteristics become evident in the initial interview. First, the most immediately noticeable characteristic of such cases is their mundane quality. In stark contrast to the histrionic personality disorder, manifestations of the schizoid personality disorder seems almost boring. Such patients present typically in an unremarkable way.

A second primary feature observed in interviewing a schizoid personality is that such individuals do not appear uncomfortable in the interview; they just appear to be aloof. The therapist can "feel" the lack of social connection by the patient's absence of appropriate social response to the therapist's attempts to make the patient comfortable initially (e.g., therapist warmth, humor, etc.).

It should come as no surprise that schizoid personality disorder cases typically have few complaints. Often, these patients suggest that the therapist speak to the significant other who has initiated the referral.

In regard to etiology, the history of the schizoid personality is typically unremarkable. Few traumas are reported. And, as the reader would undoubtedly suspect, at least one of the parents is described as being a mundane, socially introverted individual.

Clinical Experimentation

I have yet to see clinically a schizoid personality disorder case that could be formulated using the Meyer and Turkat (1979) criteria. Accordingly, clinical experimentation aimed at validating a case formulation has not been attempted.

The more typical scenario is that a hypothesis is generated to explain why there is a problem at present. Evaluation of the hypothesis depends on the nature of the hypothesis. In one case, it appeared that a senior citizen schizoid personality, whose major rewarding activity was reading, had developed a depression following progression of a visual disorder. The changes in vision appeared to now preclude reading. Administration of the Geriatric Depression scale (Yesavage, Brink, Rose, Lum, Huang, Adey, & Leirer, 1983) confirmed the patient's level of depression. Interviews of the patient and significant other confirmed a relationship between the degree of the visual problem, the inability to read, and mood disturbance. It was the effects of the patient's depression on the significant other that led to the initial referral.

Modification Methodology

Given the unsuccessful formulation of a schizoid personality disorder according to the Meyer and Turkat (1979) a priori criteria, novel clinical suggestions for intervention are not forthcoming at present. In most of these cases, I have found intervention to be dependent on the hypothesis (as opposed to a theory) about the presenting phenomena. In the case cited above, a 73-year-old married Caucasian female with no previous psychiatric history presented depression severe enough to require hospitalization by a psychiatrist. The patient's entire life seemed to fit the schizoid pattern: She did not have friends, she preferred staying by herself, she did not demonstrate the presence of strong emotions such as joy or anger, she displayed relatively constricted affect, and she spent most of her time in her home reading. In the previous year, the patient had developed macular degeneration that caused progressive deterioration of her vision, leaving her incapable of reading the types of printed books to which she was accustomed. Also about this time, her house was hit by a tornado. Thus, the two major reinforcing activities of this woman (i.e., reading and being in the security of her home) were threatened. She did not respond favorably to antidepressant medication. She eventually received electroconvulsive treatment, which significantly improved the depression. The use of large print books (available in libraries for legally but not fully blinded individuals) was found beneficial as well. This example illustrates the difficulty in applying the formulation-based approach advocated here in developing successful clinical outcomes for schizoid personality disorder cases.

SCHIZOTYPAL PERSONALITY DISORDER

The schizotypal personality disorder is characterized primarily by oddities in thought, appearance, and behavior. The DSM-III-R criteria for this disorder are provided in Table 5.4.

Individuals who have been labeled schizotypes are viewed by some as having a less severe but genetically related form of schizophrenia (APA, 1989). However, as noted in the DSM-III-R, when psychotic symptoms appear in the schizotype they are of brief duration and

Table 5.4. DSM-III-R Criteria for Schizotypal Personality Disorder

---

A. A pervasive pattern of deficiencies in interpersonal relatedness and peculiarities of ideation, appearance, and behavior, beginning by early adulthood and present in a variety of contexts, as indicated by at least five of the following:
1. Ideas of reference (excluding delusions of reference)
2. Excessive social anxiety, for example, extreme discomfort in social situations involving unfamiliar people
3. Odd beliefs or magical thinking, influencing behavior and inconsistent with subcultural norms, for example, superstition, belief in clairvoyance, telepathy, or "sixth sense," "others can feel my feeling" (in children and adolescence, bizarre fantasies or preoccupation)
4. Unusual perceptual experiences, for example, illusions, sensing the presence of a force or person not actually present (e.g., "I felt as if my dead mother were in the room with me")
5. Odd or eccentric behavior or appearance, for example, is unkempt, has unusual mannerisms, talks to self
6. No close friends or confidants (or only one) other than first-degree relative
7. Odd speech (without loosening of associations or incoherence), for example, speech that is impoverished, digressive, vague, or inappropriately abstract
8. Inappropriate or constrictive affect, for example, is silly, aloof; rarely reciprocates gestures or facial expressions, such as smiles or nods
9. Suspiciousness or paranoid ideation
B. Occurrence not exclusively during the course of schizophrenia or pervasive developmental disorder

---

Note: From American Psychiatric Association: *Diagnostic and statistical manual of mental disorders, third edition, revised.* Washington, DC, American Psychiatric Association, 1987. Reprinted with permission.

significantly less severe than in schizophrenia. The speech of the schizotype may be excessively vague or inappropriately abstract but it does not demonstrate loose associations. Although the schizotypal personality may believe in clairvoyance, he or she does not believe that his or her thoughts are being controlled by someone else. Socially anxious and eccentric, these individuals typically have few, if any, close relationships aside from immediate family members.

Interviewing the Patient

The diagnosis of schizotypal personality disorder does not seem particularly difficult because such cases routinely present as being "weird." The nature of the weirdness differs from case to case. In one clinical case the individual was demonstrating numerous ideas of reference (as opposed to delusions). A second case presented with extreme anxiety in all social interactions. Yet a third case presented as intensely vague in communicating with others.

I have noticed clinically that physical appearance/presentation attributes are often clues to a schizotypal personality disorder. In the case mentioned above involving extreme social anxiety, the patient's dress, hair style, and mannerisms were odd; but she also showed intense facial anxiety when speaking. In the case in which the individual was inordinately vague, the patient would frequently display intense eye squinting when communicating ideas that were unclear. In the case presenting ideas of reference, the patient would relate details of frightening experiences at the same time that she was smiling.

Paranoid related themes are often presented in the interview. One patient continued to feel that her husband was being pursued by another woman in her church although there was absolutely no data to support this; the patient knew this but could not change her feeling. In yet another case of schizotypal personality disorder, the patient continued to read hidden meanings into benign events. This patient lived in a rural section of a major southeastern state. When cars passed the patient's home, she read the license plates. If she saw out-of-state plates, she interpreted them as a deliberate "sign" that she was to move out of state herself.

One of the most consistent signs of a schizotypal personality disorder is that the patient's social behavior is so awkward and "weird" that it causes the individual to be uncomfortable, a state that shows also in social interchange. In one case of a gay male schizotype, the clinician was unable to determine with confidence when the patient's pauses between sentences were signals that he had finished speaking, was catching his breath, or was "taking a break." This inability of the patient to monitor his speech appropriately helped to generate his own and others' discomfort.

An important diagnostic point is that although the schizoid personality and the schizotype both have reduced social interactions, the schizotypal personality desires to have some favorable social relationships; unfortunately, the nature of such relations is awkward and uncomfortable.

Clinical Experimentation

I have yet to see the same formulation pattern across diverse schizotypal personality disorder cases. Rather, each case seems to present uniquely.

In one case of schizotypal personality disorder, the presenting complaint was pain. The formulation here was of excessive social anxiety. Accordingly, clinical experimentation involved manipulating the patient's anxiety level and determining whether changes in pain behavior occurred. The patient was monitored by galvanic skin response while anxiety was deliberately induced and eliminated. With pain ratings as a dependent variable, a clear relationship was identified between the patient's anxiety and pain level.

In a second case of schizotypal personality disorder the patient presented as "needing direction." An analysis of her difficulties led to a formulation that her problems were due to a lack of confidence in her judgment skills. To aid in the evaluation of this formulation, several norm-based reference tests were utilized. First, the formulation did not argue that the patient had an intellectual problem; rather, it seemed that she lacked confidence in her judgments. Accordingly, the patient was administered the Shipley Institute of Living Scale (Zachary, 1986). The Shipley yielded an IQ estimate of high-average intelligence. The patient was subsequently given the Wahler Self-Description Scale (1980) in which the individual rates adjectives as they apply to self-description of personality traits. It was predicted that the patient would not choose any personality characteristics at the poles (i.e., she would rate herself on adjective descriptions as being in the midrange and not at one extreme or the other, hence avoiding strong statements/judgments). This hypothesis was held even if items to be rated involved *estimating one's confidence in one's judgment skills*. The patient's performance was perfectly in line with the prediction derived from the formulation.

Given the diverse range of hypothesis and evaluation methods utilized when dealing with schizotypal personality disorder cases, the clinician's ability to generate novel ideas and to use test resources creatively is important.

Modification Methodology

At the risk of appearing redundant, it is still necessary to state that treatment designed for the schizotypal personality disorder must depend on the case formulation and not the diagnostic categorization. This treatment should also include the use of appropriate medications in select cases. In other cases, training in social skills may be the primary indicant of the formulation. Anxiety management and social skills procedures were reviewed in the paranoid personality disorder section, to which the reader is referred.

One novel intervention program that was implemented relates to the schizotypal personality disorder case mentioned above. In this example the formulation was that the patient had developed a lack of confidence in her own judgments even though there was no evidence of any difficulty with her judgment skills. In this particular case (a 37-year-old Caucasian female), a method was constructed with the patient that she could use to judge the accuracy of her judgments. First, the patient was taught that there are many levels by which to analyze any piece of information. For example, as she was staring at a plant in the clinician's office, the patient was told it could be referred to as a living organism. In that sense, the plant could be viewed in relation to numerous other organisms. At a lower level of analysis, the plant could be viewed descriptively: There is a green item in a dirt-filled container. Once the patient was able consistently to apply different levels of analyses to different items within and across item categories, she became increasingly aware that the reliability of analyses dropped as higher steps of analytic description were used. If the plant in the clinician's office were described as "a major sample of life on the planet earth compared to life that may exist on other planets," it is possible to see that this analysis is not as likely to be made by other individuals as the analysis that "this is a green entity in a dirt-filled container." Realizing that the farther she deviated from basic description, the more likely she was to make an error in judgment, she began to practice becoming a "good behavioral observer." Homework assignments included staying at the descriptive level of analysis and reading brief scientific synopses on operational description. (It was helpful that the patient was a student in a professional graduate program.)

The next stage in the treatment of this case involved teaching the patient a method of comparison for judgments. For example, if the patient was told by a significant other that she was "selfish," the patient would become extremely anxious because she was unable to judge for herself whether the description was true. Using the skills learned by being descriptive, the patient learned to evaluate such concepts in the following way. First, she was to take the concept and provide an operational definition of it. Reading a dictionary definition was often an initial step. Second, she was to describe several attributes that several other people would agree were strong indicators of that concept. Finally, the patient would look for indicators of the concept in herself. Once the patient began to acquire this skill, her schizotypal interactions were markedly diminished.

Chapter 6

Cluster B Personality Disorders

Cases of personality disorder that present clinically in dramatic fashion are grouped under the Cluster B division of the DSM-III-R personality disorder section. To refresh the reader, these include the antisocial personality disorder, borderline personality disorder, narcissistic personality disorder, and histrionic personality disorder. In contrast to the odd, awkward, or tense presentation style of Cluster A personality disorder types, individuals classified as having a Cluster B personality disorder typically provide lively mannerisms and/or content to the initial interview.

ANTISOCIAL PERSONALITY DISORDER

Without question, the antisocial personality is the most frequently researched and discussed characterological pathology in the clinical and research literature (Turkat & Alpher, 1983). Despite extensive research and clinical attention, however, most sources in the literature point to unsuccessful treatment outcome (Liebowitz, Stone, & Turkat, 1986). Intervention with the antisocial personality disorder is an unpopular topic in psychiatry (APA, 1989). Although the literature is replete with negativistic and pessimistic reports on the antisocial personality disorder, a refreshing viewpoint can be found in the work of Sutker and her associates (Brantley & Sutker, 1984; Sutker & Allain, 1983; Sutker, Archer, & Kilpatrick, 1981; Sutker & King, 1985).

In an excellent review of the literature, Sutker has argued that there are numerous myths about the antisocial personality (Brantley & Sutker, 1984). Further, Sutker (Sutker & Allain, 1983) has demonstrated that there are certain individuals in society who have antisocial characteristics yet perform successfully. Advocating open-mindedness and unbiased attitudes toward sociopaths in general, Sutker offers useful ideas for intervention with particular cases (Sutker & King, 1985).

Throughout the literature, the terms *antisocial personality*, *psychopath*, and *sociopath* have been used, often (but not always) referring to similar phenomena. For present purposes, no distinction is drawn among these terms, which are used interchangeably. The criteria for the DSM-III-R antisocial personality disorder are presented in Table 6.1.

Interviewing the Patient

Before interview tactics and observations from clinical experience are discussed, the reader should recognize that the sociopath presents clinically in diverse ways. These cases can be classified into at least three different types (which are not necessarily mutually exclusive or exhaustive). These include the *clear* sociopath, the *clever* sociopath, and the *hurting* sociopath. Each of these types presents somewhat differently and is reviewed below.

The Clear Sociopath. Diagnostically, the clear antisocial personality is the easiest to identify. Such cases may come from a court referral or an attorney, or occasionally, may be self-referred. They are referred to as *clear* because application of the DSM-III-R criteria to these cases is easily made. The patient may report that the reason for the interview is that he or she is in legal trouble and wants to learn whether the mental health professional can help him or her out of the dilemma. Although the patient may not specifically state at the outset that this is the purpose of the meeting with the clinician, it eventually becomes quite evident and the person does not deny it; in fact, the person sincerely requests the help.

The Clever Sociopath. The clever sociopath typically presents as having a "psychological problem" that is disturbing. I have seen several cases of individuals who have claimed to have heard "voices." However, careful investigation of what the individual experiences at these times shows that typically these episodes are not internally consistent nor particularly valid (e.g., the voices are neither frightening, extrinsic, or consistent with typical clinical pattern). The key is that the initial presentation of a potential clinical syndrome turns out to be a superficial presentation that is easily detected by detailed and precise investigation of the presenting complaints (i.e., use of the Behavior Analysis Matrix; see chapter 3). In such cases, the sociopath is generally attempting to manipulate the clinician to help him or her out of a particular difficulty.

Most often it is a legal dilemma, but it does not always have to be so (e.g., the individual may be seeking help in getting his or her spouse "off their back").

The Hurting Sociopath. The hurting antisocial personality is someone who meets the DSM-III-R criteria but in addition is sincerely and genuinely distressed. For example, a former Hell's Angel member, who clearly met the DSM-III-R criteria cross-sectionally and by history, was hospitalized for a multitude of significant medical problems (e.g., emphysema, neurologic disease) resulting in pain and discomfort. The patient needed to stop smoking cigarettes, drinking alcohol, and engaging in other addictive activities that worsened his medical condition. He was genuinely depressed about his dilemma. This is precisely the type of antisocial personality disorder in which Sutker's guidelines seem easy to apply. To dispense with such an individual as "untreatable because he is a sociopath" would certainly not be humane.

Interview Guidelines

Given the type of antisocial personality disorder that presents, the interview will vary considerably in tactics and content. Nevertheless, some straightforward guidelines can be offered.

First, the patient's statements should be not accepted at face value. When a point is being made, the clinician should attempt to find as much evidence as possible to support or refute the statement. If someone insists that he or she is depressed, the clinician should see a variety of symptoms that are associated with depression. If these are not evident, it is questionable whether in fact the patient has depression. In line with the recommendation not to accept statements at face value, the therapist should not accept vague reports by the patient without explanation. The more the clinician has operationalized the patient's complaint and experience, the more likely he or she is to understand the true difficulties of the patient.

The second recommendation is that the clinician should maintain honesty, acceptance, and encouragement where appropriate. Because a patient is in legal trouble does not mean that he or she should be rejected by the therapist. Rather, for the therapist to speak frankly in a warm and accepting manner and encourage the sociopath to tell the truth when it is obvious to the clinician that he or she is lying is to the patient's benefit. In this regard, the therapist can best create an atmosphere of openness and trust by being honest and understanding. In such circumstances I will often engage in appropriate "street talk" to help the patient discuss what has really brought him or her to the office.

Third, an analysis of the patient's legal history is vital as the

Table 6.1. DSM-III-R Diagnostic Criteria for Antisocial Personality Disorder

A. Current age at least 18
B. Evidence of conduct disorder with onset before age 15, as indicated by a history of three or more of the following:
   1. Was often truant
   2. Ran away from home overnight at least twice while living in parental or parental surrogate home (or once without returning)
   3. Often initiated physical fights
   4. Used a weapon in more than one fight
   5. Forced someone into sexual activity with him or her
   6. Was physically cruel to animals
   7. Was physically cruel to other people
   8. Deliberately destroyed other's property (other than by fire setting)
   9. Deliberately engaged in fire setting
   10. Often lied (other than to avoid physical or sexual abuse)
   11. Has stolen without confrontation of a victim on more than one occasion (including forgery)
   12. Has stolen with confrontation of a victim (e.g., mugging, purse snatching, extortion, armed robbery)
C. A pattern of irresponsible and antisocial behavior since the age of 15, as indicated by at least four of the following:
   1. Is unable to sustain consistent work behavior, as indicated by any of the following (including similar behavior in academic settings if the person is a student):
      a. Significant unemployment for 6 months or more within 5 years when expected to work and work was available
      b. Repeated absences from work unexplained by illness in self or family
      c. Abandonment of several jobs without realistic plans for others
   2. Fails to conform to social norms with respect to lawful behavior, as indicated by repeatedly performing antisocial acts that are grounds for arrest (whether arrested or not), for example, destroying property, harassing others, stealing, pursuing an illegal occupation
   3. Is irritable and aggressive, as indicated by repeated physical fights or assaults (not required by one's job or to defend someone or oneself), including spouse or child beating
   4. Repeatedly fails to honor financial obligations as indicated by defaulting on debts or failing to provide child support or support for other dependents on a regular basis
   5. Fails to plan ahead, or is impulsive, as indicated by one or both of the following:
      a. Traveling from place to place without prearranged job or clear goal for the period of travel or clear idea about when the travel will terminate
      b. Lack of a fixed address for a month or more
   6. Has no regard for the truth, as indicated by repeated lying, use of aliases, or "conning" others for personal profit or pleasure
   7. Is reckless regarding his or her own or others' personal safety, as indicated by driving while intoxicated or recurrent speeding
   8. If a parent or guardian, lacks ability to function as a responsible parent, as indicated by one or more of the following:
      a. Malnutrition of child
      b. Child's illness resulting from lack of minimal hygiene
      c. Failure to obtain medical care for a seriously ill child
      d. Child's dependence on neighbors or nonresident relatives for food or shelter

(continued)

Table 6.1.   *(Continued)*

---

    e. Failure to arrange for a caretaker for young child when parent is away from
       home
    f. Repeated squandering, on personal items, of money required for household
       necessities
 9. Has never sustained a totally monogamous relationship for more than 1 year
10. Lacks remorse (feels justified in having hurt, mistreated, or stolen from another)
D. Occurrence of antisocial behavior not exclusively during the course of schizophrenia
   or manic episodes

Note: From American Psychiatric Association: *Diagnostic and statistical manual of mental disorders, third edition, revised.* Washington, DC, American Psychiatric Association, 1987. Reprinted with permission.

cross-sectional examination may fail to reveal critical issues. Checking to learn whether the patient was often truant, suspended from school, or engaged in theft as a child or early adolescent is necessary for diagnostic purposes (see DSM-III-R). To obtain this information, the therapist should ask general questions: "Have you ever had any legal difficulties?" "What type of financial problems have you had?" These should be followed with more specific questions: "Have you ever been arrested?" "How many times?" "What can you tell me about your use of credit cards?" Finally, the clinician should always be guided by checking the motivation for the interview. What is it that the sociopath really wants to accomplish by seeing the mental health professional?

Unlike the schizoid personality, the antisocial personality typically provides a most stimulating interview.

Clinical Experimentation

The psychological literature describes numerous methods for diagnosing the psychopath (Brantley & Sutker, 1984). However, the approach taken in this text is to evaluate hypotheses derived from the clinician's formulation of the problem as opposed to a mere description of the problem (i.e., diagnosis). I have seen numerous clinical cases of antisocial personality disorder that could not be formulated according to the Meyer and Turkat (1979) criteria for a behavioral formulation. However, some cases can be so formulated and they typically fall into two major categories. The first is the case presenting a primary difficulty in anger control. The other presents a primary difficulty in impulse control.

In evaluating anger-related problems, the STAXI (Speilberger, 1988) provides an easily administered, scored, and interpreted norm-referenced test of state anger, trait anger, and anger expression. It is often useful to have the patient rate on a 1 to 10 scale his or her degree of anger as the therapist manipulates items that should and should not arouse and anger the patient. In certain cases, such manipulation by the therapist can be monitored by galvanic skin response or EMG response to the anger and control stimuli.

In regard to impulsivity, Zuckerman's Sensation Seeking Scale (Zuckerman, 1979) can be quite useful. Additionally, the Emotions Profile Index (Plutchik & Kellerman, 1974) provides a subscale of "dyscontrol" that sometimes proves helpful. Other useful ideas for assessing impulsivity are presented in chapter 4 in the assessment of an impulsive, narcissistic personality disorder.

Modification Methodology

In attempting treatment with the psychopath the reader is strongly advised to consult Sutker's contributions on the topic. Although I have tried to follow Sutker's guidelines in treating several cases, none of these could be viewed as fundamentally modified. However, there have been some who have benefited (in reducing their own psychological discomfort, other than "getting off the legal hook") from case formulation-based intervention.

As noted above, the two formulated primary problems have been identified in select subsets of antisocial personality disorders as those displaying anger problems and impulse control problems. Ways to control these problems are discussed below.

Anger Management. I have found clinically that the modification of anger in certain cases can be achieved easily. With the guidelines presented earlier (see the section titled "Modification Methodology" for Paranoid Personality Disorder, pp. 50–52), the bidirectional anxiety management procedures can be adapted and implemented effectively.

To start, the clinician should specify with the patient all stimuli that elicit anger. These will then be placed in a hierarchy according to the degree of anger each elicits. Whenever possible, in vivo items should be used although analogue and self-generated (e.g., imaginal) stimuli can be useful as well. After the hierarchy is constructed, a competing response such as deep relaxation or cognitive distraction should be taught and employed.

Once the responses to compete with the anger have been identified and an appropriate hierarchy has been constructed, anger management can begin. Here, the lowest level hierarchy item is presented with the instruction that at the first experience of any anger, no matter how slight, the patient will signal the therapist who will then guide the patient to invoke the competing response. The patient will signal back to the therapist when the anger has been successfully calmed. This procedure will be followed throughout the hierarchy.

Progress in anger management can be assessed by several indices. First, the therapist should measure the amount of time that elapses between presentation of the anger stimulus and signal of initial anger response. As the treatment progresses, the latency should increase until the patient has difficulty becoming angry in response to that item. Second, the clinician should measure the amount of time required to eliminate the anger once the anger-producing stimulus has successfully induced an initial reaction. Over practice trials, the time required by the patient to eliminate anger should decrease. Third, progression up the hierarchy is another indicant of anger-management success. Finally, reports on the other presenting problems that have been formulated as secondary to the anger difficulties should show improvement.

Impulse Control Training.   The development of impulse control is handled in a manner similar to that used for anger management. A hierarchy is established and the patient is taught competing responses to urges to act impulsively. The major dependent variable of interest is the patient's ability to delay acting on an impulse. In treatment, the therapist induces an urge to act impulsively and then the patient implements strategies to delay acting on that impulse for progressively increasing periods of time. A low-level hierarchy item for a particular case might require the patient to withhold giving the answer to a simple mathematical problem for increasing lengths of time. A higher level item might be to have the individual, whose "favorite cigarette" is after dinner while having a cup of coffee, experience that particular scenario but progressively delay having the cigarette.

Training of responses to compete with the impulsivity urges are typically cognitive in nature although muscular relaxation and/or bio-feedback might sometimes be useful. The most common competing responses involve *systematic distractions.* These may be classified as internal distractions or external distractions.

In *internal distraction strategies* the patient self-generates cognitions that are incompatible with the urge to act impulsively. For example, the patient may do multiplication tables, count, covertly sing a song, or systematically describe aspects of his or her immediate environment excluding the cues that elicited the urge to act impulsively. Self-rewarding statements interspersed among these activities, such as "I can handle this, see how well I am doing," can be beneficial as well.

Strategies for *external distractions* require the patient deliberately to change something in his or her immediate environment that will capture his or her attention. Such activities might involve turning on a television or radio or reading a book. The range of distraction activities is left to the ingenuity of both patient and therapist.

Indices of improvement are similar to those for management of anger and anxiety. Among these, response latencies and hierarchy progression serve as appropriate indicators of change.

BORDERLINE PERSONALITY DISORDER

The term *borderline* represents one of the major challenges and frustrations in the field of mental health. The term has been used so frequently to apply to so many different conditions, it is almost a "wastebasket" (cf. Turkat & Levin, 1984). On the other hand, while the antisocial personality disorder has received the most attention in the research literature traditionally, the DSM-III borderline personality disorder at present is the most frequently investigated characterological pathology (Gunderson, 1984). The literature is somewhat compromised, however, because often the term *borderline* does not refer to the DSM-III-R criteria but to some other problem. As noted by Widiger et al. (1988), "It is not yet clear whether borderline personality disorder describes a distinct personality syndrome, a subaffective disorder, the overlap of affective and personality disorder pathology, a level of pathology, or a heterogenic hodgepodge" (p. 790). The DSM-III-R criteria for borderline personality disorder are presented in Table 6.2.

Interviewing the Patient

Clinical cases of borderline personality disorder present in varied ways. In one case, the patient presented as wondering whether her

Table 6.2. DSM-III-R Diagnostic Criterial for Borderline Personality Disorder

---

A pervasive pattern of instability of mood, interpersonal relationships, and self-image, beginning by early adulthood and present in a variety of contexts, as indicated by at least five of the following:
1. A pattern of unstable and intense interpersonal relationships characterized by alternating between extremes of overidealization and devaluation
2. Impulsiveness in at least two areas that are potentially self-damaging, for example, spending, sex, substance use, shoplifting, reckless driving, binge eating (Do not include suicidal or self-mutilating behavior covered in [5].)
3. Affective instability: marked shifts from baseline mood to depression, irritability, or anxiety, usually lasting a few hours and only rarely more than a few days
4. Inappropriate, intense anger or lack of control of anger, for example, frequent displays of temper, constant anger, recurrent physical fights
5. Recurrent suicidal threats, gestures, or behavior, or self-mutilating behavior
6. Marked and persistent identity disturbance manifested by uncertainty about at least two of the following: self-image, sexual orientation, long-term goals or career choice, type of friends desired, preferred values
7. Chronic feelings of emptiness or boredom
8. Frantic efforts to avoid real or imagined abandonment (Do not include suicidal or self-mutilating behavior covered in [5].)

Note: From American Psychiatric Association: *Diagnostic and statistical manual of mental disorders, third edition, revised.* Washington, DC, American Psychiatric Association, 1987. Reprinted with permission.

brain had the possibility of "going dead." In another case the patient presented with having "panic attacks." In yet another case the patient presented as having bulimia. This diversity shows that the presenting complaint rarely suggests an immediate diagnostic hypothesis of borderline personality disorder. In my clinical experience, borderline personality disorders present as one of two types: those that can be formulated according to the Meyer and Turkat criteria and those that cannot. Unfortunately, the latter seem to be the greater subset. Given the vast range of pathology seen in individuals who meet the DSM-III-R criteria, this should not be too surprising.

In cases meeting the DSM-III-R borderline personality disorder diagnostic criteria, a frequently observed primary problem that ties symptoms together is that of a problem-solving deficit. However, I have found that different aspects of this basic deficiency in problem solving appear across different cases. One patient having a primary deficit in problem solving showed attributes of slow cognitive processing, a tendency to evaluate all things in a black or white fashion, and idiosyncratic attachment of valences to neutral events. In another patient with clear-cut problem-solving deficiencies, attributes of low intelligence and poor impulse control were significant aspects of the primary difficulty. In yet another case in which problem-solving ineptitude tied all symptoms together, the patient was extremely bright yet had poor frustration tolerance. Thus, when a formulation of a problem-solving deficit is hypothesized to account for the symptomatology of a particular borderline personality disorder case, the clinical correlations are likely to vary from case to case.

Given the above, it is difficult to provide clear-cut guidelines for interviewing borderline personality disorder cases according to the viewpoint specified here. However, there is no shortage of opinion on the topic; all one needs to do to affirm this is to delve into the massive literature in this area.

Clinical Experimentation

Although a useful formulation of a certain subset of borderline personality disorder cases is that of problem-solving deficiencies, hypotheses derived from the formulation for any one case will most likely yield different aspects of the problem-solving difficulty to be investigated. For example, if it is predicted that the individual has poor concept formation, administration of the Category Test (Wetzel & Boll, 1987) may prove helpful. This particular test is norm referenced and provides percentile information that can be useful. It should be noted that the Category Test is relatively sensitive to brain damage but the reader should not misinterpret the suggestion for use of this test as implying that borderline personality disorder cases are brain damaged. Rather, an evaluation of concept formation skills in and of themselves may be highly indicated.

The therapist may wish to investigate speed of cognitive processing (as referred to in one case mentioned above) in a particular clinical context. Use of the Trial Making Exam (see Lezak, 1976) provides a useful indicant of cognitive tracking speed. Measurement of psycho-motor processing speed can be achieved through use of the Symbol Digit Modalities Test (Smith, 1982). Both the Trial Making Exam and the Symbol Digit Modalities Test are easily and quickly administered, scored, and interpreted. Both are often utilized by neuropsychologists for purposes other than assessing aspects of potential problem-solving deficiencies in borderline personality disorder.

Assessment of the tendency to evaluate events in an absolute ("black and white") as opposed to a gradient (degree of "grey") manner can be readily tested by having the patient complete some type of Likert rating scale on various stimuli. The formulation-based prediction would be that there will be a high rate of extreme responses and few in the middle-rating areas. The effect may be more pronounced in certain cases of borderline personality disorder when the stimuli being rated evoke emotional responses.

The Whitaker Index of Schizophrenic Thinking (Whitaker, 1985) has subscales that may prove useful in evaluating certain ideas about borderline personality cases formulated as having problem-solving deficiencies. In one subscale, the patient is given limited information (e.g., a new alcoholic beverage has been created that affects only one side of the brain) and the patient has to choose among multiple choices the item representing the most likely immediate consequence (e.g., the drink will cost more; it will make the person partly drunk). While the clinician may not be interested in schizophrenic thinking per se, he or she may predict that on this subscale the particular borderline person-ality case should have special difficulties.

The reader has probably noticed that in almost each example given to test hypotheses with borderline personality disorder cases, the norm-referenced tests suggested are derived from areas other than the borderline personality disorder literature (e.g., literature of neuropsy-chology or schizophrenia). Always, clinical experimentation is depen-dent upon the ingenuity and skill of the clinician. The examples cited above are by no means exhaustive.

Modification Methodology

Given a formulation of a problem-solving deficit, it would appear that teaching the patient pertinent problem-solving skills would be most appropriate. Two points must be considered. First, the nature of the problem-solving deficit across cases differs and thus the treatment must differ as well. For example, if the patient has difficulty generating options, that difficulty would become the treatment focus. On the other hand, if the goal is to decrease absolute evaluation (i.e., black/white versus grey), that would require a different treatment. In certain cases, inducing a particular mood state (e.g., depression) may be most helpful when practicing problem solving. As an illustration, borderline personalities are well known for their "affective instability." In certain clinical scenarios, the therapist may have the patient focus on a videotape that induces negative affect (e.g., seeing crippled and starving children); while in this negative state, the patient would practice problem solving.

The second major point is that while a formulation of a problem-solving deficit suggests problem-solving treatment, my experience is that borderline personality disorder patients rarely allow the clinician to carry out such treatment. From session to session a new "crisis" seems to develop and often it becomes difficult to get the patient "back on track" with the basic difficulty that needs attention. Rather, the patient presents immediate demands for relief that preclude engaging in basic problem-solving practice, even when such practice might provide immediate resolution of the crisis. In this sense, while the therapist may be operating with a formulation in mind, and may have clear ideas about how to carry it out, he or she is often successfully controlled by the patient. One may find oneself engaged in doing frequent "patchwork" as opposed to the precise indicants of the formulation-derived treatment plan.

Given the above, the reader should not be surprised to learn that I have failed to change fundamentally any case that has been diagnosed as borderline personality disorder. The best clinical outcome has been a moderation of basic difficulties. In any event, several of the strategies for intervention are reviewed below.

Basic Problem-Solving Training.   A useful approach with select borderline personality disorder cases is the problem-solving format devised by Goldfried and D'Zurilla (D'Zurilla & Goldfried, 1971; Goldfried & Davison, 1976). Adaptation of this format into a flowchart to use with the patient clinically is also available (Turkat & Calhoun, 1980). This flowchart is reproduced in Table 6.3. The steps involved in problem solving are described well by Goldfried and Davison (1976), to whose work the reader is referred.

Concept Formation Training.   My experience has shown that certain patients have difficulty forming concepts. Accordingly, teaching the individual how to form a concept can be useful. The therapist may take three or four discrete, independent stimuli and ask the patient to tie

Table 6.3.   The Problem-Solving Flowchart

---

1. Identify problem (what is the problem situation?)
   a. Be as specific as possible
2. Generate all possible options (what choices do I have?)
   a. Do not judge any option
   b. Wild ideas are welcome
   c. Produce as many options as possible
   d. Combining options is acceptable
3. Eliminate any obviously poor choices
4. Examine the remaining options one at a time
   a. List all possible negative consequences of this option
   b. List all possible positive consequences of this option
   c. Eliminate option if it is generally negative
   d. Go on to next option (steps a–c)
   c. Compare all remaining options
   f. Select most positive option
5. Generate all possible ways to implement option (how can I best do this?)
   a. Use steps 2–4
6. Implement strategy to solve the problem

Note: From "The problem-solving flowchart" by I. D. Turkat and J. F. Calhoun, 1980, *The Behavior Therapist, 3,* p. 21. Copyright 1980 by the Association for the Advancement of Behavior Therapy. Reprinted by permission.

them together in some conceptual way. Often, the patient will have difficulty initially and the therapist will need to model his or her thinking strategies out loud. The patient is then encouraged to copy what has been demonstrated with a new set of stimuli. Gradually increasing the complexity of the stimuli can be useful. Of course, in the initial stages any means by which the patient forms a concept is acceptable. However, as the patient progresses, the appropriateness of the concept formulated must be more critically appraised and feedback must be provided. The reader should also note that in the speech pathology literature, there is a range of useful exercises in concept formation that are typically used for stroke victims and/or traumatic brain-injury patients; these exercises can be utilized in the manner described above for certain borderline personality disorder patients.

Categorization Management.   The tendency to evaluate problems in terms of extremes is a most difficult attribute to modify. Nevertheless, where appropriate, the therapist should provide gradual practice in learning not to evaluate events at extremes. It is critical to teach the individual to see both positive and negative features in the same item. Many borderline personalities will have extreme difficulty doing that. Modeling, shaping, and detailed instruction are helpful in teaching such patients how to moderate their tendency to evaluate events at extreme levels. When such practice exercises are given, the patient is told that under no circumstances can something be viewed as either all good or all bad. The therapist emphasizes that most events can have both positive and negative features and the patient is reinforced for attempting to outline those features in the same entity. Practice items may be as simple as looking at a picture in a magazine or as complex as evaluating the action of a positively valued significant other who engages in a disturbing activity.

Processing Speed Management.   In most cases of borderline personality disorder in which the patient appears to process information slowly, simply employing timed practice with numerous examples can often help increase the speed. For example, having the patient complete verbal mathematical problems while being timed and subsequently progressing up a hierarchy of more complex problems can often increase general processing speed. Having certain patients practice these exercises while the therapist induces specific emotional states, as noted above, can also prove fruitful at times.

As the patient becomes more adept at solving problems, the therapist becomes increasingly less of a problem solver. In this sense, the relationship to the patient changes as the patient progresses along the formulation-based treatment plan.

HISTRIONIC PERSONALITY DISORDER

The histrionic personality disorder can be considered perhaps the sine qua non of Cluster B-type characterological pathologies. Such patients present dramatically. Emotions are exaggerated in expression. Actions to capture the therapist's attention and approval are immediate and potently displayed. Whereas the schizoid personality disorder may appear mundane and the antisocial personality disorder may present stimulating content, the histrionic characterological disorder presents benign information in a highly stimulating fashion.

Often referred to as the hysterical personality, the histrionic personality has been a favorite of psychoanalytic theorists. As with so many of the DSM-III-R disorders, however, useful information for intervention purposes is lacking. Table 6.4 presents the DSM-III-R criteria for diagnosing histrionic personality disorder.

Interviewing the Patient

From a diagnostic perspective, the histrionic personality is one of the easiest characterological pathologies to identify in the clinical interview. As noted previously, the presentation of such cases is dramatic and lively. Behavior of these patients includes inappropriately exaggerated smiles and elaborate hand gestures. Movement and expression designed to please are offered continuously. Unaware of their own

Table 6.4. DSM-III-R Diagnostic Criteria for Histrionic Personality Disorder

---

A pervasive pattern of excessive emotionality and attention-seeking, beginning by early adulthood and present in a variety of contexts, as indicated by at least four of the following:

1. Constantly seeks or demands reassurance, approval, or praise
2. Is inappropriately sexually seductive in appearance or behavior
3. Is overly concerned with physical atrractiveness
4. Expresses emotion with inappropriate exaggeration, for example, embraces casual acquaintances with excessive ardor, sobs uncontrollably on minor sentimental occasions, has temper tantrums
5. Is uncomfortable in situations in which he or she is not the center of attention
6. Displays rapidly shifting and shallow expression of emotion
7. Is self-centered, actions being directed toward obtaining immediate satisfaction; has no tolerance for the frustration of delayed gratification
8. Has a style of speech that is excessively impressionistic and lacking in detail, e.g., when asked to describe mother, can be no more specific than, "She was a beautiful person"

Note: From American Psychiatric Association: *Diagnostic and statistical manual of mental disorders, third edition, revised.* Washington, DC, American Psychiatric Association, 1987. Reprinted with permission.

behavior and its effect on others, the histrionic personality demands the clinician's attention in a manner guided by the desire to please. Vague and self-centered, the histrionic personality can challenge the patience of many a skilled therapist.

Some histrionic personality disorder patients are physically attractive individuals. Unfortunately, often their social behavior decreases their overall attractiveness. It should be noted, however, although a defining characteristic of histrionic personality is the overconcern with physical attractiveness and an inappropriately sexually seductive behavior or appearance, some such patients are in fact physically unattractive. Most are unaware of the impact of their physical attractiveness/sexually seductive behavior. During the clinical interview, when a female client is asked the question, "Have you ever noticed a man showing interest in you sexually and you did not understand why?" the patient acts with astonishment at "how accurate" the clinician is.

In my clinical experience, histrionic personality disorder cases seem to fall into at least two major types: the *controlling* type and the *reactive* type.

The controlling types of histrionic personality disorder attempt to manage everyone and everything around them. These patients are concerned with getting their way and employ whatever manipulative, dramatic ploy is necessary to achieve this. In extreme cases, such individuals wreak havoc upon the institutional setting they encounter (e.g., psychiatric unit, nursing home).

In the reactive type, the histrionic personality is merely a dramatic responder to the events that unfold around him or her. The reactive type seems more guided toward seeking reassurance and approval. The controlling type is more self-centered and uncomfortable when not controlling others' attention. Both types of histrionic personalities can appear very disturbed in the extreme form.

The majority of histrionic personality disorder cases present with depression. The therapist's help is sought to decrease the immediate discomfort. Once the mood is lifted, the patient's motivation for changing is eliminated. It should come as no surprise that I am highly pessimistic about modification of histrionic personality behavior patterns.

In the formulations of such cases, a subset of these has been hypothesized to suffer from a primary deficit in empathy (Turkat & Levin, 1984; Turkat & Maisto, 1985). Unable to read others' emotions and intentions accurately, the histrionic personality remains self-centered, shallow, and uncomfortable when immediate reinforcement is not forthcoming from others. Teaching such individuals how to correct this deficiency is difficult (Liebowitz, Stone, & Turkat, 1986).

Clinical Experimentation

When there is a formulation of an empathy deficit, clinical experimentation is designed to evaluate its impact across the disordered social behavior of the individual. For example, can the patient correctly identify when someone else is having a particular emotion (i.e., social perception)? Given appropriate registration of the cue, can the histrionic personality process the information correctly (e.g., when the patient sees that someone else is unhappy, can she correctly identify the level of unhappiness experienced)? Can the histrionic personality emit the appropriate response (i.e., nonexaggerated)? Can the disordered individual profit from the indirect feedback? Unfortunately, in evaluating an empathy deficit across these four areas of social skill, I have been hard pressed to find useful norm-referenced tests. Accordingly, clinical experimentation in this regard has focused on idiosyncratically designed quasi-experiments. For example, the therapist may predict difficulty in social perception-related empathy and assess it by showing the patient pictures in magazines which the clinician believes clearly reveal an emotion; it is expected that the patient will have difficulty with such an identification. Other examples of testing an empathy deficit in histrionic personality cases can be found in Turkat and Maisto (1985).

Modification Methodology

Past experience has left me quite pessimistic about modifying the fundamental nature of a histrionic personality. The reactive type seems more amenable to change but is often remarkably less insightful than the controlling type. On the other hand, although the controlling type has insight (to a certain degree), giving up the control seems unacceptably aversive to the patient. In certain cases, one finds oneself forced to do "patchwork" as opposed to formulation-based treatment, similar to the situation with the borderline personality. However, in a subset of histrionic personality disorder cases, empathy training has been attempted—with some success in a few of these patients.

Empathy Training.   In teaching empathy to a histrionic personality, I find it useful to have the patient learn to behave like a "pseudo-Rogerian therapist." The patient is taught such basic skills as active listening, paraphrasing, and reflection. The goal is to teach the individual how to pay more attention to those around him or her and to begin to focus increasingly on others' feelings. Role playing with videotaped feedback can be highly instructive. The patient may also be assigned readings that are actually beginning therapist manuals for learning how to do Rogerian therapy.

Reaction to empathy training of this kind has been mixed. Many patients will drop out of treatment once their mood has lifted. Others conclude that the treatment is too difficult and that they do not want to learn how to focus on others' feelings anyway.

NARCISSISTIC PERSONALITY DISORDER

The literature on narcissism is impressive in quantity but specific research on the narcissistic personality disorder as defined in DSM-III is notably lacking (APA, 1989). Like the histrionic personality, the narcissistic characterological pathology is a favorite of psychoanalytic writers. A therapist has difficulty profiting from this literature, however, because the term *narcissism* may refer to many things, ranging from a level of personality organization in general to the specific characterological disorder as noted in DSM-III-R. In any event, the diagnostic criteria for the DSM-III-R narcissistic personality disorder are presented in Table 6.5. In this text, use of the term *narcissistic* refers only to the DSM-III-R personality disorder.

Interviewing the Patient

DSM-III-R notes that the narcissistic personality disorder is characterized by grandiosity, lack of empathy, and hypersensitivity to others' evaluations. It should come as no surprise that the interview behavior of such individuals is often an exercise for the patient in "showing how

Table 6.5.   DSM-III-R Diagnostic Criteria for Narcissistic Personality Disorder

A pervasive pattern of grandiosity (in fantasy or behavior), lack of empathy, and hyper-sensitivity to the evaluation of others, beginning by early adulthood and present in a variety of contexts, as indicated by at least five of the following:

1. Reacts to criticism with feelings of rage, shame, or humiliation (even if not expressed)
2. Is interpersonally exploitative: takes advantage of others to achieve his or her own ends
3. Has a grandiose sense of self-importance, for example, exaggerates achievements and talents, expects to be noticed as "special" without appropriate achievement
4. Believes that his or her problems are unique and can be understood only by other special people
5. Is preoccupied with fantasies of unlimited success, power, brilliance, beauty, or ideal love
6. Has a sense of entitlement: unreasonable expectation of especially favorable treatment, for example, assumes that he or she does not have to wait in line when others must do so
7. Requires constant attention and admiration, for example, keeps fishing for compliments
8. Lack of empathy: inability to recognize and experience how others feel, for example, annoyance and surprise when a friend who is seriously ill cancels a date
9. Is preoccupied with feelings of envy

Note: From American Psychiatric Association: *Diagnostic and statistical manual of mental disorders, third edition, revised*. Washington, DC, American Psychiatric Association, 1987. Reprinted with permission.

good I am." Some patients are shallow and superficial whereas others are actually smooth, polished, and indeed impressive. It is not uncommon for a narcissistic personality to be physically attractive as well.

The routes to therapy seem to be basically two pathways. In the first, the patient presents as being depressed because his or her relationships are not working satisfactorily. In the second scenario, the narcissistic personality disorder "wants something." For example, a successful mortgage broker who constantly had secret affairs decided to separate from his wife while at the same time manipulated her to think that he would eventually come back to her. He came to see the therapist in order to "show my wife that I am trying."

In earlier reports I was quite pessimistic about the narcissistic personality disorder (Turkat & Levin, 1984; Turkat & Maisto, 1985). However, over the years, I have gained experience with various types of this disorder and believe that there is a subset of such cases in which the patient can benefit significantly from formulation-based therapy. These types may be categorized as follows:

1. The acceptance-oriented impression-management narcissist.
2. The ruthless impression-management narcissist.
3. The self-centered impulsive narcissist.

The first type, the *acceptance-oriented impression-management narcissist*, is affected by others' behavior. The entire social repertoire of such individuals seems geared toward creating a favorable impression in others. Once this impression is created, on to the next person they go. The difficulty for acceptance-oriented impression-management narcissists is that they become incapable of "keeping up the image" with increasing contact with the same individuals. Thus, they are unable to maintain close relationships. This produces a conflict because they are desirous of having successful, close relationships. Such individuals have excellent skills at reading superficial social cues but have a true empathy deficit at the core.

The *ruthless impression-management narcissist* is also skilled at manipulating other people's evaluations of him or her. Such patients are not interested in close relationships and are so focused on manipulating others they can become ruthless. One such case was a 29-year-old female in her third marriage. This attractive and superficially polished individual revealed that should her current marital partner not provide what she desired materially and emotionally, she would have no problem "dumping him like a hot potato." It is of interest to note that the patient had been married approximately 6 weeks when she made this comment.

The *self-centered, impulsive narcissist* is exemplified by Ms. R described in chapter 4. The basic deficiency in cases like hers is the impulsivity that perpetuates the other difficulties.

Of the three types of narcissistic personality disorders, little more can be said about the ruthless impression-management type because such individuals achieve their goals after one session. The impulsive type rarely stays with treatment for a sufficient period of time for any change to occur. The case of Ms. R is a notable exception. Finally, it is the acceptance-oriented impression-management type who has the best prognosis among the three kinds of narcissistic personality disorders described.

Clinical Experimentation

Given that the ruthless type generally leaves after one session, there is no need for clinical experimentation. Examples of assessing the impulsivity of the self-centered impulsive narcissistic personality can be found in chapter 4 in the case of Ms. R as well as in ideas that have been presented in regard to the antisocial personality disorder. Some clinical experimentation guidelines for the acceptance-oriented impression-management narcissist are described below.

Several norm-referenced tests are available that the reader should find quite useful. For example, on the Emotions Profile Index (Plutchick & Kellerman, 1974) there is a subscale for "bias" that measures the patient's disposition to provide socially desirable responses. The Emotions Profile Index also has a subscale for gregariousness, which one would expect also to be significantly elevated in cases of this kind. The Social Desirability Scale, either the long form (Crowne & Marlow, 1960) or the short form (Reynolds, 1982), can also be useful. Discussions of the evaluation of empathy can be found in the clinical experimentation section on histrionic personality disorder.

Modification Methodology

Treatment of the impulsive narcissist has been described in Turkat and Maisto (1985) and follows guidelines reviewed earlier on impulse control management.

In the acceptance-oriented impression-management narcissistic personality disorder, the patient typically has excellent superficial skills in reading others' reactions. However, after inducing the appropriate impression in others, the acceptance-oriented impression-management narcissistic personality disorder really has no idea where he or she stands with others. Such patients typically do not get close enough to others to empathize adequately and to connect on strong emotions. Thus, an important goal for treatment is to teach these higher level skills of empathy.

In attempts to teach empathy of this kind, use of Rogerian-based therapist training manuals can be helpful. However, I find it useful to have the person practice being put into situations that strongly elicit emotions. In certain cases homework assignments might include visiting a crippled children's institution. Here, the patient is instructed to focus not only on the feelings he or she experiences but also to pay careful attention to the cues offered by the significant others of these unfortunate children. Patients are often encouraged to engage in charity work in which they will be forced to develop longer term relationships with individuals whose handicaps easily elicit empathy.

In line with the above, I will also assign "self-sacrifice" exercises for patients that do not immediately affect someone else's impression of them. In other words, the patient learns how to make "anonymous donations" so that other individuals are being put "ahead" of the patient; at the same time the patient is not receiving immediate reinforcement for being a "good person." Finally, reviewing interactions during an ongoing relationship between the patient and a significant other is critical for success in intervention.

Utilizing the above treatment approach, I have successfully treated a small subset of narcissistic personality disorder cases. Unfortunately, this evaluation of "success" has no scientific basis.

Chapter 7
Cluster C Personality Disorders

The avoidant personality disorder, dependent personality disorder, obsessive compulsive personality disorder, and passive aggressive personality disorder make up the Cluster C characterological pathologies in DSM-III-R. Such cases are grouped in this manner because of the anxious and fearful aspects of their personality pathology. Unlike Cluster A patients who present as weird or eccentric, or Cluster B patients who present dramatically, Cluster C personality disordered individuals seem anxious and tense.

AVOIDANT PERSONALITY DISORDER

The avoidant personality disorder, like many of its DSM-III-R counterparts, has been the subject of little empirical research (APA, 1989). Nevertheless, the problems of individuals placed in this classification present in a rather straightforward manner. The criteria for DSM-III-R diagnosis of avoidant personality disorder are presented in Table 7.1.

This type of personality pathology is characterized by timidity and anxiety concerning evaluation, rejection, and/or humiliation. The disorder is primarily anxiety based, a condition that establishes the nature of the treatment.

Interviewing the Patient

Presenting complaints of avoidant personality disorder cases typically involve one of the following three scenarios. First, the patient complains of some type of evaluation anxiety that is circumscribed in report but actually is representative of a more general problem. For example, the

Table 7.1.   DSM-III-R Diagnostic Criteria for Avoidant Personality Disorder

A pervasive pattern of social discomfort, fear of negative evaluation, and timidity beginning by early adulthood and present in a variety of contexts, as indicated by at least four of the following:
  1. Is easily hurt by criticism or disapproval
  2. Has no close friends or confidants (or only one) other than first-degree relatives
  3. Is unwilling to get involved with people unless certain of being liked
  4. Avoids social or occupational activities that involve significant interpersonal contact, for example, refuses a promotion that will increase social demands
  5. Is reticent in social situations because of a fear of saying something inappropriate or foolish, or of being unable to answer a question
  6. Fears being embarrassed by blushing, crying, or showing signs of anxiety in front of other people
  7. Exaggerates the potential difficulties, physical dangers, or risks involved in doing something ordinary but outside his or her usual routine, e.g., may cancel social plans because he or she anticipates being exhausted by the effort of getting there

Note: From American Psychiatric Association: *Diagnostic and statistical manual of mental disorders, third edition, revised.* Washington, DC, American Psychiatric Association, 1987. Reprinted with permission.

patient may seek help for a public-speaking phobia but analysis of the case reveals this to be only one small instance of a more pervasive fear of criticism and disapproval.

In the second scenario, the patient presents with depression that appears to be a consequence of the avoidant personality style.

The third route by which avoidant personality disorder cases often come to a therapist involves pain suffering. It is my experience that certain cases of gastrointestinal pain, headache, and back pain that seem tension related are often the presenting difficulties of avoidant personalities.

When the therapist is interviewing the avoidant personality case, it is critical for him or her to be accepting, nonjudgmental, and understanding. Given the patient's hypersensitivity to evaluation, an abrasive, pushy, or fast-paced therapist is likely to make the patient uncomfortable.

It is also important that the therapist be careful not to inadvertently "bulldoze" the patient into agreeing with every point made. Desiring the therapist's acceptance to an extreme, the patient is likely to fail to reveal important information or to agree that certain information is accurate when it is not, in order to gain the therapist's approval.

Finally, I believe it is important to indicate to the patient where in fact he or she "stands." Acceptance combined with frankness seems an excellent combination in general and in particular with these types of patients.

Clinical Experimentation

Evaluation of the fear of criticism and/or rejection is the primary route in clinical experimentation with avoidant personality disorder patients as most if not all of their symptoms can be tied to this basic problem. Accordingly, the Fear of Negative Evaluation Scale (Watson & Friend, 1969) is quite useful. Responses to the Social Desirability Scale (Crowne & Marlowe, 1960; Reynolds, 1982) can provide useful information as well. The Emotions Profile Index (Plutchik & Kellerman, 1974) provides a timidity subscale that might be of benefit in evaluating certain patients. Finally, presenting hypothesized anxiety stimuli while monitoring responses via galvanic skin response, heart rate, or Likert ratings often proves useful as well.

As noted above, pain complaints are often the initial presentation of the patient. Accordingly, manipulating anxiety stimuli based on a fear of evaluation and monitoring pain reactions can be especially illuminating in appropriate cases. Once the therapist has had experience with a sufficient number of avoidant personality cases to recognize them, there is little need to embark on an extensive course of clinical experimentation.

Modification Methodology

Management of the avoidant characterological disorder is relatively straightforward. Anxiety-management procedures (see earlier sections) are quite useful, particularly when the hierarchy is based on a fear of rejection, criticism, and/or evaluation. Similarly, the relationship with the patient parallels the treatment plan: initially accepting and progressively more critical as the patient develops good skills in managing anxiety.

As should be expected, the formulation of these types of cases suggests that as treatment procedures are implemented, the patient will be anxious about not performing them adequately. The therapist must keep this in mind and manage it accordingly.

Prognostically, it is my experience that such cases can be treated in a relatively short time period and in a highly responsive manner. The use of anxiolytic medications can often provide relief in a variety of such cases.

DEPENDENT PERSONALITY DISORDER

The dependent personality disorder, like the avoidant personality disorder, presents a relatively straightforward clinical picture. Such individuals are excessively anxious about making decisions and this basic difficulty perpetuates dependent and submissive behavior. The specific criteria for DSM-III-R diagnosis of dependent personality disorder can be seen in Table 7.2.

Interviewing the Patient

Like the avoidant personality, the dependent personality seeks to please, receive assurance, and be compliant. Although such patients typically do not appear as shy as the avoidant personality disorder, they are often more likely to present difficulties involving lack of initiative or inability to resolve conflicts with others.

In regard to presenting complaints, such patients do not state "I'm a dependent personality." Most do not identify decision making as a critical problem. Rather, the patient reports feeling tension or depression, which has prompted the visit to the clinician's office.

A critical variable in assessing these cases is the relationship with a dominant other. When the dominant other is available to the patient, typically there is not a problem because reassurance can always be provided. It is not uncommon in the interview for dependent personality disorder patients to state that they mold their personalities to the dominant figure with whom they are involved. However, when there is no access to a reassuring figure, the dependent personality has significant difficulty. Left to make decisions on their own, these patients experience high levels of discomfort.

Table 7.2.   DSM-III-R Diagnostic Criteria for Dependent Personality Disorder

A pervasive pattern of dependent and submissive behavior, beginning by early adulthood and present in a variety of contexts, as indicated by at least five of the following:
1. Is unable to make everyday decisions without an excessive amount of advice or reassurance from others
2. Allows others to make most of his or her important decisions, for example, where to live, what job to take
3. Agrees with people even when he or she believes they are wrong because of fear of being rejected
4. Has difficulty initiating projects or doing things on his or her own
5. Volunteers to do things that are unpleasant or demeaning in order to get other people to like him or her
6. Feels uncomfortable or helpless when alone, or goes to great lengths to avoid being alone
7. Feels devastated or helpless when close relationships end
8. Is frequently preoccupied with fears of being abandoned
9. Is easily hurt by criticism or disapproval

Note: From American Psychiatric Association: *Diagnostic and statistical manual of mental disorders, third edition, revised.* Washington, DC, American Psychiatric Association, 1987. Reprinted with permission.

Clinical Experimentation

In assessing a pervasive fear of decision making as the mechanism for the patient's presenting complaints, the Interpersonal Dependency Scale developed by Hirschfield (Hirschfield, Kellerman, Gough, Barrett, Korchin, & Chodoff, 1977) can be utilized. Further, simple manipulation of hypothesized anxiety stimuli versus control stimuli with relevant dependent measures, as outlined in previous sections of this text, can be revealing as well.

Modification Methodology

Intervention with the dependent personality disorder that has a formulated hypersensitivity to independent decision making is relatively straightforward. The general approach is bidirectional anxiety-management procedures focused on independent decision making. It is also useful to engage the cooperation of the dominant other in treatment. This cooperation is important for two reasons, especially if the patient is married. First, should the patient become less anxious about being independent, this change may have a negative effect on the relationship with the significant other. Second, assuming that the marital relationship would benefit from modification of the patient's hypersensitivity to independent decision making, the patient's progress would most likely be facilitated if the significant other were instructed in how to react, based on the patient's responses up the hierarchy. Finally, in regard to the therapeutic relationship, as the patient becomes progressively less anxious about making decisions, the therapist becomes increasingly less directive in the therapeutic relationship.

Prognostically, although there is a lack of scientific evidence on the issue, there is general agreement among clinical reporters that dependent personality disorders can be treated positively (APA, 1989). It is my experience that positive outcomes can be achieved in a relatively short period of time.

OBSESSIVE COMPULSIVE PERSONALITY DISORDER

DMS-III-R describes the obsessive compulsive personality disorder as a pervasive pattern of perfectionism and inflexibility. As can be seen in Table 7.3, such individuals are preoccupied with details, rules, and lists; they are stubborn, often workaholics, overconscientious, and inflexible regarding issues such as morality and values. These patients are often described as being stingy in affection as well as in material gifts.

The idea of an obsessive compulsive personality has been around for

Table 7.3.   DSM-III-R Diagnostic Criteria for Obsessive Compulsive
Personality Disorder

A pervasive pattern of perfectionism and inflexibility, beginning by early adulthood and present in a variety of contexts, as indicated by at least five of the following:
1. Perfectionism that interferes with task completion, for example, inability to complete a project because own overly strict standards are not met
2. Preoccupation with details, rules, lists, order, organization, or schedules to the extent that the major point of the activity is lost
3. Unreasonable insistence that others submit to exactly his or her way of doing things, or unreasonable reluctance to allow others to do things because of the conviction that they will not do them correctly
4. Excessive devotion to work and productivity to the exclusion of leisure activities and friendships (not accounted for by obvious economic necessity)
5. Indecisiveness: decision making is either avoided, postponed, or protracted, for example, the person cannot get assignments done on time because of ruminating about priorities (do not include if indecisiveness is due to excessive need for advice or reassurance from others)
6. Overconscientiousness, scrupulousness, and inflexibility about matters of morality, ethics, or values (not accounted for by cultural or religious identification)
7. Restricted expression of affection
8. Lack of generosity in giving time, money, or gifts when no personal gain is likely to result
9. Inability to discard wornout or worthless objects even when they have no sentimental value

---

Note: From American Psychiatric Association: *Diagnostic and statistical manual of mental disorders, third edition, revised.* Washington, DC, American Psychiatric Association, 1987. Reprinted with permission.

a long time although there is still considerable confusion between the Axis I disorder, *obsessive compulsive disorder,* and the Axis II difficulty, *obsessive compulsive personality disorder.* In some respects, the DSM-III seemed to help the situation by labeling the Axis I disorder as obsessive compulsive disorder and the Axis II difficulty as compulsive personality disorder. However, DSM-III-R now uses the term *obsessive compulsive* for *both* psychiatric difficulties. The problem is quite evident in the APA's own task force report on treatment (APA, 1989) in which literature on the obsessive compulsive personality disorder and obsessive compulsive disorder are confused. Clinically, the majority of obsessive compulsive personality disorder cases do not present obsessive compulsive disorder. Further, there are cases of obsessive compulsive disorder that do not meet the criteria for obsessive compulsive personality disorder. In this section, only the obsessive compulsive personality disorder is discussed. In my clinical and research experience, the literature on obsessive compulsive disorder has little if anything to do with obsessive compulsive personality disorder.

Interviewing the Patient

Initially, the obsessive compulsive personality disorder patient presents as a cooperative client. He or she is polite, unemotional, rational, and detail oriented. It is common for such individuals to complain that they are not organized enough or that they procrastinate too much. However, what becomes striking during interviews with obsessive compulsive personalities is that when asked how they feel about things, their descriptions reveal difficulty. Such patients are significantly inept at reading others' emotions and at understanding and experiencing their own. In fact, they are often proud of their "unemotionality" and their logic.

The problem is that frequently the insistence on doing things according to an unemotional, logical, rule-following doctrine angers others. Certain obsessive compulsive personality disorder types become aware of their own impact on others but do not understand it. Others seem oblivious to the negative emotions they are eliciting in others. In fact, some patients, when made aware of others' anger, point out that "they have no right to be angry." This response typifies what is wrong with the obsessive compulsive personality disorder case. Focusing on the trees, they miss the forest.

Basically, there seem to be two pathways by which obsessive compulsive personality disorder cases present themselves clinically. In the first scenario, the person is concerned that his or her productivity or cognitive skill is slipping. Most often, the patient is depressed and is complaining of an inability to be as productive as before. I have seen several retired obsessive compulsive personalities who present in their mid-70s fearing that they have Alzheimer's Disease. Actually, when tested through neuropsychological methods such as the Luria-Nebraska Neuropsychological Test Battery (Golden, Purisch, & Hammeke, 1985), they show no evidence at all of dysfunction. Such cases seem to be hypersensitive to natural changes in cognitive skills due to normal aging.

The second route by which an obsessive compulsive personality disorder case presents clinically is when someone else is concerned about the patient's behavior. For example, at the work site, the obsessive compulsive personality receives an evaluation from a superior suggesting that he or she has difficulty getting along with others. However, the patient often fails to grasp the impact of his or her own behavior on others. In certain cases, the obsessive compulsive personality is angered by the accusations because they are seen as being false.

From a formulation-based perspective, there is a subset of obsessive compulsive personality disorder cases whose presenting complaints can be formulated as due to being excessively rational. Other cases cannot be so easily formulated.

Finally, when such patients are interviewed, they appear to be most comfortable when the interaction is as organized, detail oriented and unemotional as possible.

Clinical Experimentation

A variety of methods can be employed in clinical experimentation with obsessive compulsive personality disorder cases, depending on the needs of the particular clinical situation. For certain patients, evaluation of anger responses particularly when things do not go their way can prove useful. In these cases, projective tests, particularly those that emphasize expression of feelings (e.g., the Geriatric Sentence Completion Form by Le Bray, 1980) often predict concrete unemotional answers. Another interesting variant in clinical experimentation is to have the patient rate the degree of discontent he or she experiences when reviewing materials that induce emotions compared with materials that do not induce emotions.

A variety of patients will present clinically as having cognitive difficulties. A patient may complain that there is something wrong with his or her memory or concentration. Sometimes depression is the cause of it, but whether or not the person is depressed, often the patient will insist upon being assured that nothing is wrong with their thinking skills. At such times the therapist might administer neuropsychological tests such as the Luria-Nebraska Neuropsychological Test Battery (Golden et al., 1985), Symbol Digit Modalities Test (Smith, 1982), the Weschler Memory Scale Revised (Weschler, 1987) and the Stroop Color-Word Exam (Golden, 1978) for concentration. Almost invariably, such patients are found to be performing at high levels for individuals in their age group.

Modification Methodology

I have found that the majority of obsessive compulsive personality disorder cases I have seen are unable to profit from the type of treatment advocated in this text. Many patients will agree with a formulation that they are excessively rational, but they are fearful of engaging in treatment that they perceive will "strip away their strength." When these patients are presented with ideas for gradually increasing their pleasure and emotion-related experiences while decreasing their over-zealous work commitment—even if the ideas are presented in a cautious, gradual manner—most patients balk at the suggested treatment. Occasionally, a small number are willing to attempt such treatment and can improve significantly. Gradually increasing pleasure and emotional experience, decreasing work commitment, and teaching sensitivity to others' feelings are often reported by this subset of patients to be of significant benefit in decreasing their excessive rationality.

I have seen several depressed obsessive compulsive personality disorder cases that respond well to antidepressant medication. However, I have yet to see such a case modify his or her personality traits under such a treatment regimen.

PASSIVE AGGRESSIVE PERSONALITY DISORDER

The passive aggressive personality disorder is described in DSM-III-R as being characterized by a pervasive pattern of passive resistance to demands for performance. The individual may procrastinate, complain, or forget as indirect expressions of resistance. The specific criteria for diagnosis are presented in Table 7.4.

Interviewing the Patient

Based on my clinical experience, there are two major types of passive aggressive personality disorder cases. In the first and most common, the patient does not see himself as having a problem; someone else has "forced" him to come for therapy. Additionally, the patient has minimal if any insight (or perhaps fails to admit) that he or she is in fact a major part of the problem. An example is an insulin-dependent adolescent who deliberately "forgets" to monitor her blood glucose. This behavior infuriates the mother who is an overly controlling person.

In the second type of passive aggressive personality disorder, the

Table 7.4. DSM-III-R Diagnostic Criteria for Passive Aggressive Personality Disorder

---

A pervasive pattern of passive resistance to demands for adequate social and occupational performance, beginning by early adulthood and presenting in a variety of contexts, as indicated by at least five of the following:
1. Procrastinates, for example, puts off things that need to be done so that deadlines are not met
2. Becomes sulky, irritable, or argumentative when asked to do something he or she does not want to do
3. Seems to work deliberately slowly or to do a bad job on tasks that he or she really does not want to do
4. Protests, without justification, that others make unreasonable demands on him or her
5. Avoids obligations by claiming to have "forgotten"
6. Believes that he or she is doing a much better job than others think he or she is doing
7. Resents useful suggestions from others concerning how he or she could be more productive
8. Obstructs the efforts of others by failing to do his or her share of the work
9. Unreasonably criticizes or scorns people in positions of authority

---

Note: From American Psychiatric Association: *Diagnostic and statistical manual of mental disorders, third edition, revised.* Washington, DC, American Psychiatric Association, 1987. Reprinted with permission.

individual presents vaguely. One patient stated that he sought therapy because "I just felt like I wasn't getting anywhere." This type of case appears less frequently. Unfortunately, passive aggressive personalities who refuse to view themselves as a major part of their own problem are unwilling to participate in the therapy process. I have seen several cases of passive aggressive personality disorder in which the patient presented as a "medical" patient who was driving his or her significant other "crazy." Unfortunately, the patient continued to attribute all the difficulties to the medical condition and did not accept psychological explanations.

In the type of case in which patients seek help for themselves, the range of passive-resistance activities is wide and includes "I have a bad memory," "It takes me awhile to do things," "I am not as sharp as he is." In one case, a passive aggressive personality's initial complaint was that he had a problem with his memory. Administration of the Weschler Memory Scale Revised (Weschler, 1987) revealed that the patient had a superior memory; he scored at the 98th percentile for someone in his age group.

In the subset of treatable cases, the patient often has an assertiveness deficit due to a fear of negative consequences for being expressive. Typically, the patient was reared by one if not two dominating parents who punished the patient for any expression of disagreement or negative emotion. The patient learned to resist passively. Unfortunately, when the patient moved on to other relationships in life, these skills remained, interfering with successful relations.

Clinical Experimentation

It is important to be able to rule out the patient's "excuses" for his or her difficulties. Demonstrating that the patient has no problem with memory often can be an important assessment target. On the Rathus Assertiveness Schedule (Rathus, 1973), such patients are often predicted to score low on assertion in regard to emotion-related situations but high on assertion regarding non-emotion-related situations. In other words, certain passive aggressive personality disorders are viewed as having an assertiveness deficit specific to condition and not a generalized assertiveness problem. For example, in complaining about a steak in a restaurant, the passive aggressive individual typically has no difficulty. However, in a disagreement with a significant other that will lead to negative emotion on the significant other's part, the patient has enormous difficulty being expressive. Evaluation of the patient's anxiety is as critical as assessment of the social skills necessary for him or her to be able to express emotion directly. Unfortunately, there is no easily administered norm-referenced test to assess social skills; therefore idiographically designed clinical experimentation is in order.

Modification Methodology

Individuals who have a passive aggressive personality and are formulated as having significant deficiencies in direct expression of emotion seem to respond well to a modification methodology involving the following components. First, the therapist will identify all avoidances and anxiety stimuli and deal with them according to the anxiety-management protocols detailed previously in this text. Second, he or she will identify areas of known passive aggressive behaviors to use in role playing, with the patient practicing in a graduated fashion, the opposite position. Finally, the therapist will develop a hierarchy of behaviors for self-initiation and help the patient to carry them out in a gradual manner.

From a therapeutic relations standpoint, it is important for the therapist to not be so dominant as to arouse passive aggressive reactions in the patient. However, it is also important that he or she not be inordinately passive as the patient may be too uncomfortable in taking the initiative. The therapist needs to calibrate his or her interactions with the patient according to the progress of the individual along these dimensions.

Part III
Future Issues and Applications

Chapter 8
Professional Responsibilities

The preceding pages have stressed the lack of research information on highly prevalent psychopathologies such as the character disturbances. The personality disorders, given new prominence in the DSM-III and DSM-III-R editions, remain primarily the province of the clinician. Although the amount of research activity devoted to the personality disorders has increased tremendously since the introduction of DSM-III, this research has yet to provide meaningful guidelines for clinical practice. Calling for more research is appropriate but insufficient. What is needed is some fundamental changes in the way that clinicians and researchers interface. This chapter presents an outline of various approaches to this topic.

SCIENTIST-PRACTITIONER MODEL

The scientist-practitioner model has been discussed extensively over the years but its role in clinical work has been limited usually to the clinician as a consumer of research finding. One of the most common descriptions of the scientist-practitioner is the clinician who utilizes scientific theory and data to guide his or her practice. For several reasons this seems to be a rather limited view of how the scientist-practitioner operates in the clinical arena. If we were to treat only those disorders for which strong scientific evidence was available to support psychological intervention, we would have to turn away the vast majority of individuals seeking our help. In fact, prominent clinical researchers such as Robert Spitzer, MD, and Stanley Rachman, PhD, are in agreement that only a handful of disorders have strong scientific evidence to support intervention (APA, 1989; Rachman & Wilson, 1980; Spitzer & Williams,

1985). What then should be done when we see patients clinically presenting disorders that have yet to be shown scientifically to be amenable to change?

First, we should try to provide the best possible treatment we can given the lack of scientific data available. However, there is an additional obligation that falls upon us as scientist-practitioners. This obligation can best be understood in the context of the process of science itself.

Process of Science

Science operates on ideas. Without hypotheses to test science does not proceed, and the fate of most hypotheses is to die within the process of science. Accordingly, what is most needed is a multitude of useful, novel hypotheses about psychopathology. It is in this area that clinicians can play a valuable role in the scientific enterprise. There is no better example than Freud of how clinical ideas catalyze research activity. None of us is likely to make such a high-level contribution. Nevertheless, there is a variety of things in the everyday practice of clinicians that can contribute significantly to the scientific literature as well as help us fulfill our broader obligations as scientist-practitioners. Before outlining these activities, it is important to specify what clinicians should not be expected to do as contributors to science.

Limitations of Clinicians in the Scientific Process

Clinicians cannot be expected to conduct research that allows a strong inference. The reasons are straightforward. First, experiments require standardization and control; however, there are too many variables operating in the clinical arena to permit this type of study in most cases. Second, in some research, deception of or withholding treatment from subjects would be necessary. This is clearly unacceptable for ethical clinical practice. Finally, clinicians do not have the luxuries of time, manpower, energy, and resources to conduct experimental research. So what can the clinician do? The answer has been well illustrated in other fields (cf. Turkat, 1988).

Many of the advances in medicine have come from observations and hypotheses contributed by physicians in their private offices. Much scientific understanding of medical pathology would never have come about without these original hypotheses and quasi-testing of them by medical practitioners. Another example is in the area of bird song. Today there is considerable scientific understanding of the nature of bird song. However, this knowledge would never have been amassed without the reports of devoted backyard amateurs who recorded observations and hypotheses. In the same way, mental health clinicians can help to expedite the growth of scientific knowledge of psychopathology.

CLINICAL CONTRIBUTION TO THE SCIENTIFIC LITERATURE

There are five different activities that even the privately practicing clinician can utilize to contribute to the scientific literature. These are the descriptive case study, case theory report, case theory investigation, case treatment report, and case treatment investigation.

Descriptive Case Study

Clinicians are presented frequently with disorders about which there is not only minimal research available but also very few useful clinical reports. In such situations, it is useful for clinicians to provide a descriptive case study. Here, the clinician characterizes the clinical features and/or etiology of a poorly understood disorder. For example, fugue states are minimally researched disorders in which useful clinical reports are lacking. When a clinician is presented with such a case, his or her description can be informative for others in the field. By describing these patients cross-sectionally and/or providing historical information of relevance, clinicians could provide a significant contribution to the literature. Assume for the moment that 10 clinicians around the country who saw fugue states in a particular year each provided such a description. Assume further that some common patterns emerged from these descriptions. These 10 descriptive case studies would provide a useful basis for a researcher to develop hypotheses to be evaluated in the next step of the research process.

Case Theory Report

The case theory report involves presentation of a clearly defined formulation of a particularly case. For example, the literature on paranoid personality disorder (Turkat, 1985), devoid of research data and replete with generally pessimistic clinical speculations, offers little assistance to the clinician. When presented with such a case, if the clinician is able to generate a formulation that can be clearly defined and communicated to other professionals, it would be a valuable addition to the literature.

Case Theory Investigation

A third activity for clinicians is the case theory investigation. This refers to a clearly defined formulation that is presented along with a quasi-experimental test of its validity. An example of a case theory investigation can be found in Turkat and Maisto (1985).

Case Treatment Report

The essence of a case treatment report is a description of an innovative treatment. An example is Turkat and Carlson's (1984) synopsis of an innovative treatment for modification of dependent personality disorder. Its value has been noted elsewhere (APA, 1989).

Case Treatment Investigation

A fifth activity for therapists in contributing to the scientific literature is the case treatment investigation. Here an innovative treatment is systematically evaluated. An excellent example is the report by Adams, Malatesta, Brantley, and Turkat (1981) in which a case of schizophrenia was conceptualized as the consequence of an attention deficit. Various tests were employed to evaluate the effects of a treatment designed to teach attentional skills. The case was treated in just nine, 50-minute outpatient sessions and gains were maintained at follow-up.

ADDITIONAL RESPONSIBILITIES

In addition to writing up appropriate clinical cases, clinicians can participate in the scientific process. For example, the DSM-III and DSM-III-R field trials invited contributions by interested clinicians. As we approach the DSM-IV, under the leadership of Allen Frances, MD, clinicians can play a helpful role in sorting out personality pathologies.

An additional useful activity for therapists involves direct communication with researchers. When clinicians come across research articles that pertain to cases with which they feel they have expertise, they should communicate with the investigators. These contacts can be most helpful in transmitting information from one sphere to the other.

In light of these and other points made, researchers must come out of their "ivory towers" to accept the limitations of clinicians, identify their strengths, and seek their input. With such openness, optimism, and opportunity, it is likely that the growth of knowledge in psychopathology will be expedited.

Chapter 9
Concluding Comments

In the preceding pages, one approach to the DSM-III-R personality disorders was described and illustrated. Clinical knowledge generated by this application was reviewed as well. Implications for the approach in regard to generating new knowledge, particularly from the clinical arena, were outlined. However, a number of issues in regard to the personality disorders as well as the psychological approach described need to be addressed.

First, the DSM-III-R has its problems and these are quite evident in clinical practice. In clinical settings it appears that many cases are unlikely to fit one particular personality disorder description. It is more often the case that the patient presents phenomena that merit classification as a personality disorder *not otherwise specified*. The reason for this is that with the change in diagnostic criteria, numerous cases seem to fit several personality disorder criteria descriptions. It is relatively common in clinical settings to hear a case described as "a Cluster B-type personality disorder" rather than with a primary DSM-III-R pathological disorder label. Research has begun to confirm this difficulty in diagnostic overlap.

In a related investigation, Blashfield and Breen (1989) compiled a list of each diagnostic criterion for all the personality disorders in DSM-III-R. They provided these lists to clinicians who were asked to determine the specific disorder with which a particular criterion was associated. The order of presentation was scrambled and clinicians were instructed not to refer to the official APA diagnostic manuals. The results of this study indicated that the average clinician assigned only 66% of the criteria to appropriate categories. Not only did this study raise questions about the face validity of the DSM-III-R personality disorders, but it also demonstrated a high degree of overlap in the use of criteria for many of the personality disorders. Blashfield and Breen (1989) concluded that "these results suggest that either the meanings ascribed to the criteria for these disorders by DSM-III-R do not match the meanings as understood by American clinicians or the wording of many criteria is unclear" (Blashfield & Breen, 1989, p. 1579).

Another issue that was not addressed in the preceding pages was the novel introduction of the self-defeating personality disorder and sadistic personality disorder in the DSM-III-R. There were many who pushed to include these two disorders as part of the official DSM-III-R personality disorder section. However, a decision was made to leave the number and types of DSM-III-R personality disorder categories constant with those of the DSM-III but to include the self-defeating personality disorder and sadistic characterological disorder in the appendix, as "worthy" of further investigation. Analysis of the evaluation process by which it was decided to include or exclude these personality pathologies is certainly of interest. As an example, the reader is encouraged to examine the results of a national field trial of the criteria for self-defeating personality disorder (Spitzer, Williams, Cass, & Davies, 1989).

In addition to the DSM-III-R personality disorders themselves, some final comments should be offered regarding the application of the particular psychological approach presented in this text to these disturbances. As the reader undoubtedly noticed, many personality disorder cases can be formulated according to the Meyer and Turkat (1979) criteria. However, many cannot. In the latter case, the clinician still operates within the same framework but is limited to creating *hypotheses* accounting for less of the clinical data. In such instances, the clinician has more restricted guidance in carrying out his activities with the particular case given the absence of a *theory* about the patient. Even so, I still believe that the approach in general advocated herein is of significant value in clinical work even with cases in which the full Meyer and Turkat (1979) criteria cannot be met. As illustrated by activities in which the clinician can participate in the scientific process (see chapter 8), a hypothesis-testing approach to clinical work offers much to the practicing clinician (Turkat, 1988). It is my hope that the reader will find the material in this volume to be constructive in future clinical and research endeavors on the personality disorders.

References

Adams, H. E. (1981). *Abnormal psychology*. Dubuque: Wm C Brown.

Adams, H. E., Malatesta, V., Brantley, P. J., & Turkat, I. D. (1981). Modification of cognitive processes: A case study of schizophrenia. *Journal of Consulting and Clinical Psychology, 49,* 460–464.

American Psychiatric Association. (1952). *Diagnostic and statistical manual of mental disorders.* Washington, DC: Author.

American Psychiatric Association. (1968). *Diagnostic and statistical manual of mental disorders* (2nd ed.). Washington, DC: Author.

American Psychiatric Association. (1980). *Diagnostic and statistical manual of mental disorders* (3rd ed.). Washington, DC: Author.

American Psychiatric Association. (1987). *Diagnostic and statistical manual of mental disorders* (3rd ed., rev.). Washington, DC: Author.

American Psychiatric Association. (1989). *Treatments of psychiatric disorders: A task force report of the American Psychiatric Association.* Washington, DC: Author.

Barlow, D. H., & Hersen, M. (1984). *Single case experimental designs* (2nd ed.). Elmsford, NY: Pergamon Press.

Blashfield, R. K., & Breen, N. J. (1989). Face validity of the DSM-III-R personality disorders. *American Journal of Psychiatry, 146,* 1575–1579.

Brantley, P. J., & Sutker, P. B. (1984). Anti-social behavior disorders. In H. E. Adams & P. B. Sutker (Eds.), *Comprehensive handbook of psychopathology* (pp. 439–478). New York: Plenum Press.

Carey, N. P., Flasher, L. V., Maisto, S. A., & Turkat, I. D. (1984). The a priori approach to psychological assessment. *Professional Psychology, 15,* 519–527.

Cattell, R. B. (1946). *The description and measurement of personality.* New York: Harcourt Brace Jovanovich.

Ciminero, A. R., Calhoun, K., & Adams, H. E. (1986). *Handbook of behavioral assessment* (2nd ed.). New York: Wiley-Interscience.

Crowne, D. P., & Marlowe, D. (1960). A new scale of social desirability independent of psychopathology. *Journal of Consulting Psychology, 24,* 349–354.

Davidson, P. O., & Costello, C. G. (1969). *N = 1: Experimental studies of single cases.* New York: Van Nostrand Reinhold.

D'Zurilla, T., & Goldfried, M. (1971). Problem solving and behavior modification. *Journal of Abnormal Psychology, 78,* 107–126.

Endicott, J., & Spitzer, R. L. (1978). A diagnostic interview: The schedule for affective disorders and schizophrenia. *Archives of General Psychiatry, 35,* 837–844.

Feighner, J. P., Robbins, E., & Guze, S. B. (1972). Diagnostic criteria for use in psychiatric research. *Archives of General Psychiatry, 26,* 57–63.

Golden, C. J. (1978). *Stroop color & word test.* Chicago: Stoelting.

Golden, C. J., Purisch, A. D., & Hammeke, T. A. (1985). *Luria-Nebraska neuropsychological battery: Forms I & II manual.* Los Angeles: Western Psychological Services.

Goldfried, N. R., & Davison, G. C. (1976). *Clinical behavior therapy.* New York: Holt, Rinehart & Winston.

Guise, B. J., Pollans, C. H., & Turkat, I. D. (1982). Effects of physical attractiveness on perception of social skill. *Perceptual & Motor Skills, 55,* 19–22.

Gunderson, J. G. (1984). *Borderline personality disorder.* Washington, DC: American Psychiatric Association.

Hersen, M., & Barlow, D. H. (1976). *Single case experimental designs.* Elmsford, NY: Pergamon Press.

Hirschfield, R. A., Kellerman, G. L., Gough, H. G., Barrett, J., Korchin, S. J., & Chodoff, P. (1977). A measure of interpersonal dependency. *Journal of Personality Assessment, 41,* 610–618.

Lachar, D. (1980). *The MMPI: Clinical assessment and automated interpretation* (6th ed.). Los Angeles: Western Psychological Services.

Le Bray, P. R. (1982). *Geriatric sentence completion form.* Odessa, FL: Psychological Assessment Resources.

Lezak, M. D. (1976). *Neuropsychological assessment.* New York: Oxford University Press.

Liebowitz, N. R., Stone, N. H., & Turkat, I. D. (1986). Treatment of personality disorders. In A. J. Frances & R. E. Hales (Eds.), *American Psychiatric Association annual review* (Vol. 5, pp. 356–393). Washington, DC: American Psychiatric Press.

Malatesta, V. J., Aubuchon, P. G., Bloomgarden, A., & Kowitt, M. P. (1989). Hospital based behavior therapy services. *The Psychiatric Hospital, 20,* 119–123.

Meyer, V., & Reich, B. (1978). Anxiety management: The marriage of physiological and cognitive variables. *Behavior Research & Therapy, 16,* 177–182.

Meyer, V., & Turkat, I. D. (1979). Behavioral analysis of clinical cases. *Journal of Behavioral Assessment, 1,* 259–270.

Millon, T. (1981). *Disorders of personality. DSM-III: Axis II.* New York: John Wiley & Sons.

Morey, L. C. (1988). Personality disorders in DSM-III & DSM-III-R: Convergence, coverage and internal consistencies. *American Journal of Psychiatry, 145,* 573–577.

Persons, J. B. (1989). *Cognitive therapy in practice: A case formulation approach.* New York; W W Norton.

Platt, J. R. (1966). Strong inference. *Science, 146,* 347–353.

Plutchik, R., & Kellerman, H. (1974). *Emotions profile index.* Los Angeles: Western Psychological Services.

Pretzer, J., & Fleming, G. B. (1989). Cognitive behavioral treatment of personality disorders. *The Behavior Therapist, 12,* 105–109.

Rachman, S. J., & Wilson, G. T. (1980). *The effects of psychological therapy* (2nd ed.). Elmsford, NY: Pergamon Press.

Rathus, S. A. (1973). A thirty-item schedule for assessing assertive behavior. *Behavior Therapy, 4,* 398–406.

Reynolds, W. N. (1982). Development of reliable and valid short forms of the Marlowe-Crowne Social Desirability Scale. *Journal of Clinical Psychology, 38,* 119–125.

Robins, L. N., Helzer, J. E., Croughan, J., & Ratcliff, K. S. (1981). National Institute of Mental Health diagnostic interview schedule: Its history, characteristics, and validity. *Archives of General Psychiatry, 38,* 381.

Schachter, S., & Rodin, J. (Eds.). (1974). *Obese humans and rats.* Potomac, MD: Lawrence Erlbaum Associates.

Smith, A. (1982). *Symbol digit modalities test.* Los Angeles: Western Psychological Services.

Spielberger, C. D. (1988). *State-trait anger expression inventory*. Odessa, FL: Psychological Assessment Resources.

Spitzer, R. L., & Williams, J. B. W. (1985). Classification of mental disorders. In H. I. Kaplan & B. J. Sadock (Eds.), *Comprehensive textbook of psychiatry* (4th ed., 591–613). Baltimore: Williams & Wilkins.

Spitzer, R. L., & Williams, J. B. W. (1987). Introduction to DSM-III-R. In American Psychiatric Association, *Diagnostic and statistical manual of mental disorders (3rd ed., rev.)*. Washington, DC: American Psychiatric Press.

Spitzer, R. L., Williams, J. B. W., Cass, F., & Davies, M. (1989). National field trial of the DSM-III-R diagnostic criteria for self-defeating personality disorders. *American Journal of Psychiatry, 146,* 1561–1567.

Sutker, P. B., & Allain, A. N. (1983). Behavior and personality assessment in men labeled adaptive sociopaths. *Journal of Behavioral Assessment, 5,* 65–79.

Sutker, P. B., Archer, R. P., & Kilpatrick, D. G. (1981). Sociopathy and antisocial behavior: Theory and treatment. In S. M. Turner, K. S. Calhoun, & H. E. Adams (Eds.), *Handbook of clinical behavior therapy*. New York: John Wiley & Sons.

Sutker, P. B., & King, A. R. (1985). Antisocial personality disorder. In I. D. Turkat (Ed.), *Behavioral case formulation* (pp. 115–153). New York: Plenum Press.

Thompson-Pope, S. K. & Turkat, I. D. (1988). Reactions to ambiguous stimuli among paranoid personalities. *Journal of Psychopathology & Behavioral Assessment, 10,* 21–32.

Thompson-Pope, S. K., & Turkat, I. D. (1989). Paranoia about paranoid personality research. *Journal of Clinical Psychiatry, 50,* 310.

Turkat, I. D. (1979). The behavior analysis matrix. *Scandinavian Journal of Behavior Therapy, 8,* 187–189.

Turkat, I. D. (1982). Behavior-analytic considerations of alternative clinical approaches. In P. Wachtel (Ed.), *Resistance: Psychodynamic and behavioral approaches* (pp. 251–257). New York: Plenum Press.

Turkat, I. D. (1985). Formation of paranoid personality disorder. In I. D. Turkat (Ed.), *Behavioral case formulation* (pp. 161–198). New York: Plenum Press.

Turkat, I. D. (1986). The behavioral interview. In A. R. Ciminero, K. S. Calhoun, & H. E. Adams (Eds.), *Handbook of behavioral assessment* (2nd ed.) (pp. 109–149). New York: Wiley-Interscience.

Turkat, I. D. (1987). Invited case transcript: The initial clinical hypothesis. *Journal of Behavior Therapy & Experimental Psychiatry, 18,* 349–356.

Turkat, I. D. (1988). Issues in the relationship between assessment and treatment. *Journal of Psychopathology and Behavioral Assessment, 10,* 185–197.

Turkat, I. D., & Alpher, V. (1983). An investigation of personality disorder descriptions. *American Psychologist, 38,* 857–858.

Turkat, I. D., & Alpher, V. (1984). Prediction versus reflection in therapist demonstration of understanding: Three analogue experiments. *British Journal of Medical Psychology, 57,* 235–240.

Turkat, I. D., & Banks, D. S. (1987). Paranoid personality and its disorder. *Journal of Psychopathology & Behavioral Assessment, 9,* 295–304.

Turkat, I. D., & Brantley, P. J. (1981). On the therapeutic relationship in behavior therapy. *The Behavior Therapist, 4,* 16–17.

Turkat, I. D., & Calhoun, J. F. (1980). The problem-solving flowchart. *The Behavior Therapist, 3,* 21.

Turkat, I. D., & Carlson, C. R. (1984). Symptomatic versus data based formulation of treatment: The case of a dependent personality. *Journal of Behavior Therapy & Experimental Psychiatry, 15,* 153–160.

Turkat, I. D., & Kuczmierczyk, A. R. (1980). Clinical considerations in anxiety management. *Scandinavian Journal of Behavior Therapy, 9,* 141–145.

Turkat, I. D., & Levin, R. A. (1984). Formulation of personality disorders. In H. E. Adams & P. D. Sutker (Eds.), *Comprehensive handbook of psychopathology* (pp. 495–522). New York: Plenum Press.

Turkat, I. D., & Maisto, S. A. (1983). Functions of and differences between psychiatric diagnosis and case formulation. *The Behavior Therapist, 6,* 184–185.

Turkat, I. D., & Maisto, S. A. (1985). Application of the experimental method to the formulation and modification of personality disorders. In D. H. Barlow (Ed.), *Clinical handbook of psychological disorders* (pp. 503–570). New York: Guilford Press.

Turkat, I. D., & Meyer, V. (1982). The behavior-analytic approach. In P. Wachtel (Ed.), *Resistance: Psychodynamic and behavioral approaches* (pp. 157–184). New York: Plenum Press.

Turner, S. M., & Turkat, I. D. (1988). Behavior therapy and the personality disorders. *Journal of Personality Disorders, 2,* 342–349.

Wahler, H. J. (1980). *Wahler self-description inventory.* Los Angeles: Western Psychological Services.

Watson, D., & Friend, R. (1969). Measurement of social evaluation anxiety. *Journal of Counseling and Clinical Psychology, 43,* 384–395.

Wechsler, D. (1987). *Wechsler memory scale revised.* San Antonio: The Psychological Corporation/Harcourt Brace Jovanovich.

Wetzel, L., & Boll, T. J. (1987). *Short category test, booklet format.* Los Angeles: Western Psychological Services.

Whitaker, L. (1985). *Objective measurement of schizophrenic thinking: A practical and theoretical guide to the Whitaker index of schizophrenic thinking.* Los Angeles: Western Psychological Services.

Widiger, T. A., Frances, A., Spitzer, R. L., & Williams, J. B. W. (1988). The DSM-III-R personality disorders: An overview. *American Journal of Psychiatry, 144,* 786–795.

Wolpe, J., & Turkat, I. D. (1985). Behavioral formulation of clinical cases. In I. D. Turkat (Ed.), *Behavioral case formulation* (pp. 5–36). New York: Plenum Press.

Workgroup to revise DSM-III. (1985). Draft: *DSM-III-R in development.* Washington, DC: American Psychiatric Association.

World Health Organization. (1979). *Manual of the international statistical classification of diseases, injury, and causes of death* (9th rev.). Geneva: Author.

Yesavage, J. A., Brink, T. L., Rose, T. L., Lum, O., Huang, V., Adey, N., & Leirer, V. O. (1983). Development and validation of a geriatric depression screening scale: A preliminary report. *Journal of Psychiatric Research, 17,* 37–49.

Zachary, R. A. (1986). *Shipley institute of living scale.* Los Angeles: Western Psychology Services.

Zuckerman, M. (1979). *Sensation seeking: Beyond the optimal level of arousal.* Hillsdale, NJ: Lawrence Erlbaum Associates.

Author Index

Subject Index

About the Author

Ira Daniel Turkat received his Ph.D. in clinical psychology at the University of Georgia in 1980. He completed his doctoral internship at the Middlesex Hospital Medical School of the University of London. Dr. Turkat has served on the faculties of Vanderbilt University School of Medicine, University of North Carolina at Greensboro, and the University of Florida College of Medicine. He is an internationally known expert in the fields of behavior therapy and the personality disorders. He has published over 70 journal articles, book chapters, and books and has served as an editorial consultant for numerous journals including the *Journal of Consulting and Clinical Psychology, Behavior Therapy,* and *Science.* He is the Associate Editor of the *Journal of Psychopathology and Behavioral Assessment,* which is received in 25 countries worldwide.

Psychology Practitioner Guidebooks

Editors
Arnold P. Goldstein, Syracuse University
Leonard Krasner, Stanford University & SUNY at Stony Brook
Sol L. Garfield, Washington University in St. Louis

J. Kevin Thompson—BODY IMAGE DISTURBANCE: Assessment and Treatment

William J. Fremouw, Maria de Perczel & Thomas E. Ellis—SUICIDE RISK: Assessment and Response Guidelines

Arthur M. Horne & Thomas V. Sayger—TREATING CONDUCT AND OPPOSITIONAL DEFIANT DISORDERS IN CHILDREN

Richard A. Dershimer—COUNSELING THE BEREAVED

Eldon Tunks & Anthony Bellissimo—BEHAVIORAL MEDICINE: Concepts and Procedures

Alan Poling, Kenneth D. Gadow & James Cleary—DRUG THERAPY FOR BEHAVIOR DISORDERS: An Introduction

Ira Daniel Turkat—THE PERSONALITY DISORDERS: A Psychological Approach to Clinical Management